ITALIAN WESTERN
The Opera of Violence

ITALIAN WESTERN

The Opera of Violence

by Laurence Staig and Tony Williams

Lorrimer

© Laurence Staig and Tony Williams 1975
First Published in 1975 by Lorrimer
Publishing Limited 47 Dean Street London
W1 in association with Futura Publications
Limited 110B & C Warner Road London SE5

ISBN 0-85647-059-7

Origination in Great Britain by
Jack Pia Limited London

Designer: Dave Allen
Cover design: JWA Designs

Printed in Great Britain by
Hazell Watson & Viney Ltd,
Aylesbury, Bucks

The authors and publishers wish to thank the following for their help: Allessandro Allessandroni for his kind hospitality in Rome, the British Film Institute Education and Information Departments whose reputation for patient forebearance and courtesy is well deserved, Bruno Bianchi of CAM Dischi, Giancarlo Bongiovanni, Carlo Bixio of Cinevox, Christian and Mimi Berthaud, Brenda of Beat, Enzo Cocumarolo, Francesco De Masi, Golden Era, Giusseppe Giacchi, Guadagno Giovanni, Michael 'I've run out of 2ps' Jones, Paul Lech as inspiration for a 'Sabata' still, Sergio Leone, Miracle Films, Monthly Film Bulletin, Luciano Morello, Gordon McWee, Ennio Morricone for his kind hospitality, Sergio Pagoni of Gemelli, Alexander Persluz, Lula Sarchioni, Barbara Tiger for the interview photographs and the stripes, Alan Warner of United Artists, Tony Watts – Director of the 1975 Thames Polytechnic Festival, Sheila Wayling for her very kind help as technical interpreter in Rome, and Irving Wilson of EuroBeat.

CONTENTS

PART I
ITALIAN WESTERN

The Ecstasy of Violence

'Where Life had no value
Death sometimes had its price.
That is why the bounty hunters appeared.'

Introductory prologue from
For a Few Dollars More

At its highest expression, the world of the Italian Western is that of an insecure environment of grotesqueness abounding in almost surrealistic dimensions, in which Violence reigns. The locale is that of the early period of the West, when it was in process of formation; this leads eventually towards the final stage envisaged in Leone's *Once Upon a Time in the West*. The hero (or main protagonist, since there are strictly speaking no 'heroes' in the moral dramatic sense in the Italian Western), is an individualist, who is scruffy and unshaven; he continually smokes a cigar or cheroot, and he is outside the boundaries of the American Western's accepted society. He can only survive by playing by the arbitrary rules of the system in which he finds himself or by

Tomas Milian in *Django Kill!*

making his own rules. He must adapt to whatever new circumstance arises. His way is brutal, as there can be neither gentleness nor compassion in the world which he inhabits. Thus Eastwood murders his wounded adversaries after the duels from which he has emerged the victor. Tomas Milian in *Django Kill!* can do nothing but acquiesce in the murder of an innocent boy by Roberto Camardiel and his henchmen. These are the rules of the game in the dimensional existence of the Italian Western, in which to lose means obliteration and to win means doing so by all the savage means at one's disposal.

There can be no friendship or trust in such a situation. Only a temporary uneasy truce is possible as long as both sides see the

advantage of a common alliance. It may be broken at any time as the multifarious alliances and double crossings of Eastwood and Wallach in *The Good, the Bad and the Ugly* illustrate. If the main protagonist ever rides off into the sunset in the classic American Western manner it is usually with tragic dimensions as seen at the end of *The Avenger* when Nero rides off with the body of his younger brother. In *Drop Them or I'll Shoot (The Specialist)* Hallyday departs, mortally wounded, spurning the love and security offered by Silvy Fennec who may also be seen as a threat to his isolated individuality by leading to his possible integration into the corrupt community which he has saved. At the climax of *Once Upon a Time in the West* the camera focuses on Cardinale offering water to the cosmopolitan gang of railroad construction workers, who are bringing the advantages of civilisation to the West. The camera then scans to the right, viewing the departing figures of Bronson and the dead Robards ignored by the figures of this new era. Cardinale has survived the events of the film and will continue to enjoy the benefits of the new civilisation, in which there is now no place for the men of the West as exemplified by Fonda, Bronson and Robards.

It is this picture which we will find throughout the whole genre of the Italian Western, in good and bad products but exemplified to good effect by the masters and competent directors in this field. There are fluctuations of course. Many of the films are unwatchable and several either imitate the American Western or use certain of its motifs to make their own contributions, as illustrated in this latter respect by Carlo Lizzani's *The Hills Run Red* and Duccio Tessari's *A Pistol for Ringo* and *The Return of Ringo*. It is a world which is antithetical to what may be described as the established field of the American Western. Although we must note that such a field may be hard to define now, both due to continuing critical study opening out the ideas of exponents of this genre and its continuing change under influences of other ideas, chief of which has been the Italian

Eastwood and Wallach in *The Good, the Bad and the Ugly.*

Western. In spite of the fact that some examples of the latter may be fine organised contributions to the overall picture of the Western itself and others may be disorganised and gratuitous there can be no doubt that in its day the Italian Western injected a fresh note of realism and enthusiasm into the American Western tradition, which was in danger of becoming sterile. Though directors such as Anthony Mann and Budd Boetticher are now recognised to have been key innovators in the period of the 50's and early 60's, as works such as Jim Kitses' *Horizons West* illustrate, it must be noted that the US Western as such was under the dominant oppression of clichés which hindered any real progress being made within the genre itself. Admirable though the concepts in the work of Mann and Boetticher may have been it must be recognised that they worked within the standard definition of the Western. Despite critical articles which may be written about *The Tin Star,* for example, it cannot be denied that it has the form of a Saturday morning Western with black and white morality, of clean-shaven heroes and swarthy villains. The Italian Western does not have the optimistic frontier tradition of the films of John Ford, or the defined qualities of certain of Howard Hawks' Westerns such as *Red River.* Frequently the hysterical cry of 'John Ford would not have made something like this!' has been raised against the Italian Western. Of course not, since Ford was a product of his own cultural heritage and would have been incapable of making an Italian Western, as an Italian director would have been unqualified to make a John Ford Western. Note that in *Once Upon a Time in the West* Leone contents himself with a visual homage to Monument Valley, then departs to his own thematic concepts knowing full well the impossibility of imitating that director. It has been argued that the works of Ford, Mann and Boetticher constitute the true genre of the Western as such and that any deviations should be disregarded. The assumption

Hallyday in *Drop Them or I'll Shoot.*

Giuliano Gemma in *The Return of Ringo*.

often is that only Americans can make Westerns and that all that has been said on Westerns has been said by the above trinity. However this not only clashes with the fact that directors such as Fritz Lang have made excellent Westerns, but also that Western directors such as Walsh, Wyler and Zinneman are by no means one hundred per cent American. Sergio Leone is a renowned authority on the history of the Old West. Henry Fonda commented once in an interview that Leone knew more about the West than most American directors. One example of the use of his knowledge in his films may be seen in *The Good, the Bad, and the Ugly* with the accurate depiction of the uniform of the Union troops, with correct period cannon and artillery mobilised in authentic formation, just before the futile battle of the bridge. Like most forms of cinematic expression the Western is continually evolving and it is absurd to say that all that can be said on it has been said by a few critically regarded American directors.

We have cited Ford and others as examples of the best tradition of the American Western, but it must not be forgotten that in addition to what may be defined as the best examples of the genre there were often innumerable duds. The Western in the American cinema has always been seen as entertainment fodder open to competent, average and below average director alike, to be exploited for commercial ends. Despite the efforts of William S. Hart to depict his

frontier locations as they actually were, the general effect was to substitute individual initiative for cliché. Thus elements foreign to the American era were projected on to it – the Republicanism of John Wayne, American small town values, Mom's apple pie, and gaudy, as opposed to realistic, costumery. Though the dance motif was an essential part of several of Ford's Westerns such as *Wagonmaster* and *The Searchers* where it expressed the solidarity of the community it was often done to death by inferior directors thus unfortunately becoming a well-worn cliché. The Indian, the 'original American' was frequently there to be wiped out despite the efforts of *Broken Arrow* and *Cheyenne Autumn* to go against the tide. The Mexican was also to be despised as villain or figure of fun. Clean cut

heroes with angelic morality predominated and the Western went into a decline from which it has never wholly freed itself. *The Monthly Film Bulletin,* 25, 1958, p.117 has a review of the Western *Quantrill's Raiders* with a comment which could apply to many of the standard Westerns produced in the forties and fifties: 'Some of the film's obviousness can be gathered from the way in which the good men are all clean shaven while the villains are never seen without a messy stubble on their chins'. The Western was used as a vehicle of the star system and Cagney, Bogart and Gable were some of the many who made Westerns without consideration of whether they were suited to the field in the first place. Cardboard heroes arose such as Tom Mix and Hopalong Cassidy and the genre reached

Pierre Brice as Winnetou in *Apaches Last Battle*.

its all-time low with the 'singing cowboys' – Roy Rogers, Gene Autry and Tex Ritter. It is true that attempts were made at realism and innovations were tried but not until *The Wild Bunch, Will Penny* and a few other films did the genre begin to recover. But would *The Wild Bunch* ever have been made had it not been for the influence of the Italian Western?

It is not our purpose to criticise here the whole genre of the American Western or to argue for the total superiority of the Italian model. As will be shown the Italian

Western had a very high proportion of bad works which often threaten to submerge the distinctive works of the field. What we are arguing for is an unbiased critical assessment of the Italian Western. More often than not it has been dismissed solely on the grounds of its 'un-American' nature and as being simply entertainment fodder. Though this snobbishness of ignoring a film made for a mass audience might have been thought to have died since the heyday of *Cahiers du Cinema*, one still finds it resurrected against the Italian Western. True it belonged in form to one of the Italian film industry's commercial boom cycles during 1964–70. However, contempt for the Italian tradition of jumping on the bandwagon of cinematic genres such as the epic, the crime thriller and the Western – which in many cases can be quite justified – is a false attitude, particularly when it fails to evaluate properly the attempts of any director to provide something new in a particular genre and avoid the second-rate pastiche. Colin McArthur has persuasively argued that as the crime films of Jean-Pierre Melville have enlarged the gangster film arena in a masterly sense so the films of Sergio Leone have given a much needed booster shot into the arm of the Western. No serious film critic would dismiss Le Samourai, Le Cercle Rouge, or the magnificent Le Deuxieme Souffle with the derisory comment of 'garlic gangster film' and ignore them because they are un-American. Any film genre such as the horror film, the gangster film or the Western has its abundance of cheap imitations which rub off on to the original works. Thus a true critical perspective and lack of bias is seriously needed to discern the works of merit. Likewise the now defunct Italian Western undoubtedly had a total of ninety per cent dross but within the remainder lies the work of directors such as Leone, Sollima and Corbucci, Petroni, Questi and Damiani to which attention must be drawn.

The continental Western did not begin with the Italian interest in the genre. It had a long sporadic history going back to the silent era, but the Italian boom began soon after the German film industry adapted the Western stories of Karl May, which were built around the characters of Old Shatterhand and Winnetou. There the American Western clichés were often renewed under a new guise as any viewing of Winnetou the Warrior and Among Vultures will show. Spain had been making Westerns in the traditional manner as Gunfight at High Noon (1963) and The Gunfighters of Casa Grande (US/Spain, 1964) will show. Italy had been making Westerns before the beginning of the definitive

Italian product in 1964 but there is little likelihood that Ride and Kill (1963), Buffalo Bill, Hero of the Far West (1964), or Le Pistole non Discutono (1964) were of any special interest as Westerns. Indeed the non-serious product such as Rita in the West (1967) starring pop singer Rita Pavone was in evidence after the new work of Leone in 1964-5. However, the Italian Western must be seen in relation to the commercial Italian film industry's interest in profitable film genres; and it must not be forgotten that it was the same interest in genres such as 'sword and sandle' involving heroes such as Hercules, Goliath, Ursus and Maciste that was the basis for the flood of Westerns made between 1964–70. It has been a common tendency for critics to view these films disdainfully regarding them with the same sort of contempt they had for the B-film not many years before. The idea that working on a commercial film is beneath any artist of distinction does not seem to exist in Italy as much as in the rest of the Western world. Important artists such as Patroni Griffi, Carlo Lizzani and Damiano Damiani can work in the commercial field occasionally without it being regarded as prejudicial towards their getting any work of consequence in the future. Indeed a look at the 'sword and sandle' or 'musclemen' genre will be instructive as we shall see several familiar names who would soon become involved in the developing Italian Western field.

At the beginning of the epic, genre names like Leone, Corbucci, Tessari were present, but once the field began deteriorating they moved on to other concerns. Leone made his first appearance as director in 1959 with the Italian-Spanish co-production of the re-make of The Last Days of Pompeii, a Steve Reeves spectacular. He even collaborated on the script with Ennio de Concini, Luigi Emmanuele, Duccio Tessari and Sergio Corbucci. At the time the film had a bad review castigating the dubbing but one line was prophetic. 'Strung on to a story fit for a Western or a gangster film is a series of bloody and incredible adventures designed to exhibit the muscles of Steve

Reeves . . .' At least three of the script-writers were later to move on to the Western. That *Monthly Film Bulletin* review, however, was typical of contemporary critical opinion which seemed to slam the Italian epics mainly because they were not American. Critics were oblivious of the fact that the Italians were really the forerunners of that genre and comments were full of the same prejudices which were later to be exhibited against the major Italian Westerns. At the time the writer remembers that these films were no better or no worse than their American counterparts. Indeed they were more fun and this was the intention of the Italian film industry – to make epic films of commercial mass appeal full of humour and healthy irreverence for the actual genre itself. In addition to the above-mentioned names, figures like Mario Bava directed films such as *Hercules at the Centre of the Earth* (1961) and *Fury of the Vikings* (1961). He was later to make the Westerns *La Strada per Fort Alamo* (1964) and *Roy Colt and Winchester Jack* (1970). Massimo Dallamano, later to be director of photography on Leone's first two Westerns, acted in the same capacity on *Constantine the Great* (1960), Damiano Damiani, meanwhile, co-scripted *Herod the Great* (1960) from a story on which he had collaborated, and in the same year co-scripted *Cleopatra's Daughter*. In 1961 Sergio Corbucci had directed two examples of the genre – *Goliath and the Vampires,* which he co-scripted with Tessari – and *Duel of the Titans,* a story which had been contributed to by Leone. Sergio Sollima had collaborated on the script of *Goliath against the Giants* (1961) which had two actors in the cast who were to be particularly active in the Western – Fernando Rey and Fernando Sancho. At this time Giuliano Gemma was a leading juvenile who appeared at the tail end of the cycle before going on to the Western. In 1962 he had starred in the irreverent *The Titans* which was directed by Tessari and in the following year co-starred in *Goliath and the Sins of Babylon*. Composers later to become active in the Western such as Carlo Rustichelli and Francesco de Masi were also

present. The list of collaborations is endless. Thus the Italian Western was begun by many artists who had worked in the old epics and was therefore an essentially commercial concern from the first. It was certainly not an art form to appeal to any intellectual minority. If it be held that any commercial concern cannot be deemed worthy of consideration then this ignores standards of contemporary film evaluation. A director has as much chance of making a really important film in a commercial area as he has in the limited 'art' definition. Realisation of this fact has now resulted in a correct appreciation of the American films of Fritz Lang and the individuality of directors such as Sam Fuller and Nicholas Ray. Even in the early sixties some English critics grudgingly recognised the distinctiveness of artists such as Cottafavi, Bava and Freda who were more highly regarded in France than here. In reference to the Western a greater realism and extension of the genre is seen in the political motif entering into the script of these films. It is often forgotten that writers of the stature of Franco Solinas have scripted or written the stories for certain Westerns. Only recently has the Leone Trilogy been shown in The National Film Theatre, and after the misunderstanding and bias has gone, then the way will be open for a more objective understanding of Italian Western directors.

As well as acknowledging the indebtedness of the Italian Western to the genre which preceded it, we must also see it within the wider context of the Italian cinema. If it is a mistake to judge the whole mood and context of the Indian cinema by the films of Satyajit Ray, so also is it wrong to hold that the films of a Visconti or Antonioni sum up the Italian cinema. In Italy, as in India there is a vast popular audience, and the Italian Western was designed to serve the needs of this audience for escapist entertainment. In the silent era many epics abounded and as any popular cinema is the reflection of the mood of the country involved so the Italian Western reflected an essentially Italian reinterpretation of the Old West. Reflections

Burt Reynolds in *Navajo Joe*.

Bret Halsey and Tatsuya Nakasai in *Today It's Me . . . Tomorrow You!*

Ernest Borgnine and George Hilton in *Vengeance is Mine*.

of a highly volatile emotional temperament, proud of family life, reverent to religion and quick to avenge any insult to family life or person by vendetta, are the qualities we see. The Western for Italy, thus did not reflect the frontier-building hardiness of the pioneers of the American West, which was mediated in the US cinema by means of the realistic tradition of narrative film with which critics are generally familiar. Rather the Italian Western had a less understated delivery and reflected more an existential, almost romantic image which involved the spectator wholly in the actions on screen. Thus the emphasis would be primarily on the visuals and soundtrack, in which the emotions of the audience would be captured. It can be no accident that one of the most frequent motifs in the Italian Western is that of the vendetta. Colonel Mortimer sets out to avenge his sister's death on Indio in *For a Few Dollars More*. Joe conducts a ruthless revenge for the murder of his wife and tribe in *Navajo Joe*. Bill Kiowa pursues the man who framed him and murdered his wife in *Today It's Me — Tomorrow You* while John Warner nurtures his deadly hatred of Sandoval who indirectly, out of his stubborn racialism, has caused the death of his wife and child

in *Vengeance is Mine*. Ringo must avenge the death of his father, the betrayal of his wife, the loss of honour of an American town at the hands of the Mexicans and at the same time regain his own identity in *The Return of Ringo*. John Philip Law pursues the murderers of his family in *Death Rides a Horse,* with only a few key images of their deaths in his mind planted there when he was young; while Franco Nero avenges the honour of his murdered father and violated mother in *The Avenger*. At its extreme Joseph Cotten pursues a vendetta against the Union for the defeated South in *The Hellbenders,* refusing to accept as final the verdict of the Civil War. The list is endless but it is interesting to note how much the vendetta motif is linked with the family, and how the thin veneer of civilisation on the part of the avenger often breaks down into a ruthless lust for the enemy's death.

With deep concerns such as this, there can be no wonder why the tenor of the Italian Western is emotional, at times perhaps too emotional, for the audience of Britain and America. This existential dimension inherent in a film, which is foreign to an English audience — except in the ways it is manipulated in weepies, women's films

John Phillip Law in *Death Rides a Horse*.

From *10,000 Dollars Blood Money*.

and controlled swashbucklers of Hollywood manufacture – may explain the hostility with which critics have greeted it. The hideously bad dubbing in many cases works against the genre and it is the fault of the distributors for having allowed this. In many cases the distinctive style of Italian acting is ruined. Fortunately Leone's films and a fair proportion of the better examples of those of Sollima, Corbucci and Tessari have escaped this but others have been seriously ruined. However despite this, audiences have welcomed the films because they are a fundamental part of the cinema of adventure, designed to appeal to a mass audience, luring them away from the cares of everyday life, providing a cathartic therapy to the feelings of frustration in a mechanised society. As a purely Italian product originally made for the Italians it has a unique style of acting which seems extravagant and flamboyant to an English audience. It is important to accept the acting for what it is, otherwise the whole point of the film may be lost. Thus the death of Joseph Cotten in *The Hellbenders* may seem grotesque and laughable to an audience which has still not shaken off the 'stiff-upper lip' tradition of British cinema entirely. Understood in its filmic context, however, it is an integral part of the film, reiterating by visual motifs the collapse of

the Southern cause, Jonas' sanity and the death of the family unit expressed in a manner almost akin to that of Greek tragedy. Furthermore the death of Gian-Maria Volonté in *Face to Face* when he crawls up a sand dune and disappears after he has been shot by Milian may likewise seem absurd, but again this is part of the Italian expressionist mode of acting. It symbolises Brad's defeat, his utter isolation from the forces of law and civilisation he had once purported to represent and from the growing moral awareness of the once savage Beau. Brad is lost and perplexed at Beau's action. His disappearance from the scene of action now prepares the way for Sollima's essential dialectic of the politics of law and justice which Siringo (William Berger), like most Sollima 'law-abiding' figures, has to decide on.

Humour has also been an important feature of the Italian cinema. It has not only been confined to straight forward comedies, but has entered into all spheres of cinematic concern. The Roman tradition of satire lives on in the Italian cinema, as it sends up even the most revered of institutions, as in the ecclesiastical fashion parade in Fellini's *Roma*. Corbucci himself directed a send-up of Visconti's *The Leopard* in *Il Figlio del Leopardo* in 1965. Tessari's ability to satirise elements of the genre in which he is working appeared to good effect in *A Pistol for Ringo* as well as in the humorous interludes between Ringo and his infant daughter in *The Return of Ringo*. The tension in *For a Few Dollars More* is relieved by an incident in a saloon between Lee Van Cleef and Klaus Kinsky, in a manner reminiscent of the best traditions of silent film comedy. With Leone it is a fixed episode and is not allowed to intrude into the rest of the film as he is one of the few directors to have total control of satire and humour in his work. The collaboration between Eastwood and Wallach in *The Good, the Bad and the Ugly* is also reminiscent in its way of classic screen comedy partnerships of straight man and fall guy until the film enters a more serious vein. Steiger in *A Fistful of Dynamite*

has a humour born of naïveté which is lost when his family suffer the cost of his alliance with the world-weary John (James Coburn). The Trinity films with Terence Hill are a gentle dig at the classic conventions of the American and Italian Westerns. In the Leone produced *My Name is Nobody,* Hill himself performs a classic comedy routine in a contest involving his accuracy with a gun under the influence of liquor. Used competently and sparingly within the broad compass of a film, this element can contribute highly to it, but in the hands of lesser directors undue baroqueness and vulgarity mar the film. *For a Few Bullets More,* for example, treads the borderline between an interesting satire of themes of the Italian Western and just plain awful direction.

From *Vengeance is Mine.*

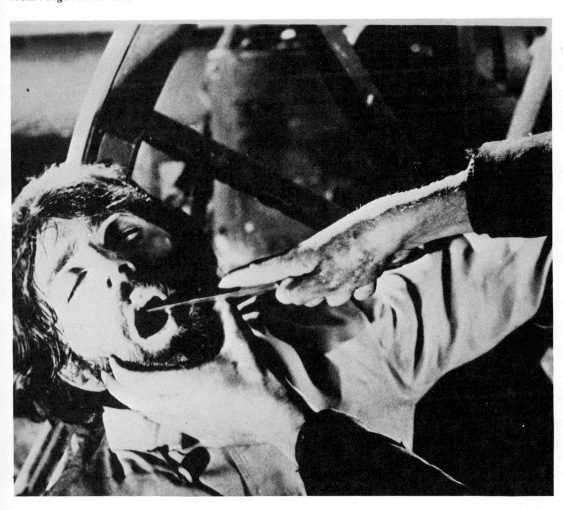

From *Death Rides a Horse*.

One of the most common elements of the Italian Western has been its use of violence. A number of anonymous heroes answering to the names of Ringo, Django, Sartana, The Stranger or No-Name at all appear as main protagonists in a battleground of violence. Only one thing interests them – gold. Attempts made to connect these figures with their prototypes in the epic genre such as Hercules, Goliath and Ursus fail when comparison is made with the Western. Whereas those heroes belong to the age of mythical heroism, performing deeds of valour to rescue maidens from wicked kings or monsters, the Italian Western hero generally has his own interests at heart, stooping to the most violent means possible. It cannot be denied that in the hands of competent directors such as Leone and Sollima, violence has contributed to the mood of the film and resulted in a far greater realism than the old static conventions of the American Western allowed. The Old West was a very violent place and insecure for many as any history book on the period attests. When No-Name is beaten up by Ramon's men in *A Fistful of Dollars* he is actually *seen* to have been brutally beaten. It is not the old convention of a trickle of blood from the side of the mouth and dishevelled hair which has been the common stock effect in many American Westerns. Likewise the murder of the family by Indio in *For a Few Dollars More* and the breadwinners of another by Angel Eyes in *The Good, the Bad and the Ugly,* shock us more by emphasising the raw nature of the frontier of that time and reiterating the insecurity of the family unit. Likewise in *Once Upon a Time in the West* we have the murder of the McBains. In the Dollar Trilogy No-Name kills his wounded adversaries. Brought up in the clean tradition of the American Western this shocks us until we later objectively reflect that this is the code of the West and that no man would live long if he acted otherwise. It is a lesson which Frank Talby (Lee Van Cleef) impresses on Joe Mary (Giuliano Gemma) in *Day of Anger* which is to rebound ironic-

Van Cleef and Gemma in *Day of Anger*.

The Minister in *Find a Place to Die*.

The Monk in *Vengeance is Mine*.

ally on him. Brett Halsey and Franco Nero both shoot their enemies to death in *Today It's Me – Tomorrow You* and *The Avenger* while Gemma begins the process with George Martin in *The Return of Ringo*. All these men have suffered from their enemies. Vengeance will result in a catharsis for them, a removal of the malignant growth unless as in the case of Harmonica in *Once Upon a Time in the West* they are already inwardly dead. It is true that the violence can be carried to excessive lengths by some directors but it is a mistake to tar the whole genre with the label of gratuitous violence and not investigate each particular case to see whether it was more justified in some than in others. As we have emphasised, one of the benefits of the Italian Western has been in bringing a greater degree of realism to the depiction of the Old West. Without the innovations of the Italian Western it is doubtful if the violence of Peckinpah's *The Wild Bunch* would ever

have been acceptable. Leone himself, has refuted the charges of gratuitous violence claiming that he is telling a fable in a realistic style. Life is full of violence and his films merely reflect this but there can be no denying Leone's claim for his films having a cathartic effect. Many films have been much more violent. Clint Eastwood has emphasised this in several interviews. The 'Stranger' films of Tony Anthony with the vast majority of bandwagon-jumping films have undeniably been guilty of this. But in any field there has always been the case of the untalented majority attempting to better the success of a talented innovator, by using in excess the elements he has used in controlled moderation. So, objective examples and less generalised accusations should be the rule rather than the exception.

Violence is exhibited in pursuit of the only reality in the Old West and that is money. Possession of it is the only guarantee of power and pursuit of it, normally by illegitimate means, is the only way for the hero. It is a fact of life that most men act from motives of greed and venality, and the positive value of the Italian Western is to illustrate this, despite the awkward ways in which it does so. The American Frontier is shown to have been built up from these motives. This is in opposition to the American Western's frontier-building imagery of integrity and honesty most exemplified by Cecil B. De Mille.

With the three qualities of greater emotionalism, humour and violence we have just discussed, it is obvious that to understand whether they have been used properly or just as a gimmick, we have to investigate the film itself. Our comments only serve as tentative general summaries. The difference between Italian Western hero and that of the American Western is that the former is an outsider, who unscrupulously plays by the rules of whatever special environment he finds himself in. This is necessary for his survival. The aim he has in mind is either revenge or acquisition of money, by legitimate or illegitimate means. No-Name is a bounty killer achieving his aim by being an outsider in areas where the law cannot penetrate. By contrast the American Western hero is usually clean-cut, clean-living, regulating his conduct by the law and Holy Book. If Steve Judd in Peckinpah's *Guns in the Afternoon* wishes to 'enter his house justified' the Italian Western hero is under no such illusions about the power of these elements. Religion is either powerless — as in *For a Few Dollars More,* and *The Good, the Bad and the Ugly* — or impotent as in *Death Rides a Horse* and *Once Upon a Time in the West* where Cheyenne leads the vigilante churchgoers into a desert it would take them days to get out of. It may also be discarded by its own representatives as with the sadistic rapist minister in *Find a Place to Die* and the disillusioned monk in *Vengeance is Mine* who joins John Warner's gang. The most cynical depiction of its uselessness is in *No Room to Die* where William Berger appears in the role of the black-garbed, compulsive, bible-reading bounty killer —

Preacher: In a period of violence it can not flourish. At best it is a cloak to hide behind, an escape from the realities of everyday existence, as the character of Father Ramirez (Luigi Pistilli) in *The Good, the Bad and the Ugly* shows. The healthy superstition of Tuco (which appears at odd moments only when his interests are at stake, such as the threatened death of No-Name) is at least preferable to the hypocritical façade of his brother. While John Warner and his gang are hunted by Mexican soldiers, a religious procession occurs from nowhere. Peculiarly enough in the Italian Western it is only the religion of a minority group which is respected. In *The Big Gundown* and *They Call Me Trinity* it is the Mormon community which takes in figures who are outcasts from civilised society. While on the run from Corbett, Cucillo (Tomas Milian) is offered shelter by the Mormons and he is accepted as one of them, so much so that a fourteen-year-old Mormon wife is left alone with him. This is in contrast to the suspicion of Cucillo engendered elsewhere in the film. Trinity (Terence Hill), one of the most unkempt heroes the Italian Western has ever produced, is welcomed into the Mormon community with his brother Bambino (Bud Spencer). As before there is no suspicion of the two. However, this favourable depiction of the Mormons may be due to the fact that in the historical period of the early West, they too were regarded as outcasts. The institution of the law is not respected in the Italian Western. No-Name deposes the corrupt sheriff in *For a Few Dollars More.* In *Today It's Me — Tomorrow You!* the inability of the law to help Bill Kiowa in the quest for his wife's murderer is illustrated by the sheriff resigning to join Kiowa's band and appointing the town drunk in his place.

Another important theme given emphasis is that of the outcast. The Italian Western has given a greater dignity and understanding to this figure than most conventional Westerns. Unlike Corbett (Lee Van Cleef) it is Cucillo who is more aware of the corruption present in the circles of civilisa-

tion which Corbett represents. Sollima constructs *The Big Gundown* by depicting Cucillo as a degenerate murderer whom Corbett has to hunt; but gradually we begin to appreciate him as an individual, rough and grotesque though he may appear. He has fought with Juarez but is pessimistic about the New Mexico he has attempted to build. However he can always evade Corbett in the chase and he proclaims his superiority right to the end of the film. Navajo Joe (Burt Reynolds) is the last survivor of a dead race in a land snatched up by rapacious capitalism. The town despises him, but he is the only one who can save them from a gang of killers. Corbucci represents the theme of oppression in three examples in the film: the town, the gang and the Indian girl. The town is the representative of the new civilisation which despises the old inhabitants of America as inferior beings, but it is deluded by the crooked husband of the banker's daughter. The gang of scalphunters are also outcasts paradoxically oppressing the Indians, but the psychopathic hatred of its leader (Aldo Sambrell) for the Indians is due to the fact of his being a half-breed himself, a fact brought out by his conflicts with his fair-haired younger brother. It is emphasised in *Navajo Joe* that the only place for the Indian now in the new America is either being at the mercy of the scalphunters outside the town or accepting second-class status by selling out their ancient heritage. This is exemplified in the figure of the Indian girl (Nicoletta Machiavelli). Ironically it is Joe who saves the town at the cost of his life, though he asserts his dignity by accomplishing his vendetta. He is the last survivor of the great past of the Indian, left in a society in which he has no established place. The outcast theme is also seen in *The Hellbenders,* another Corbucci film. Jonas (Joseph Cotten) and his family of Southerners are outcasts in the Civil War aftermath. Despite his murderous efforts in a futile attempt to revive the Southern cause Jonas can be seen as a figure of tragic dimensions. His cause is already lost and his

The Bandit as outcast from *The Big Gundown*.

The Family as outcasts from *The Hellbenders*.

The Bounty Hunter from *The Good, the Bad and the Ugly.*

sons are either cynical or doubtful about the whole venture. The most well-known representative of the outcast figure is, of course, Tuco (Eli Wallach). He has come to terms with the facts of life – one must become either a priest or a bandit. His way is more honest paradoxically than that of his sanctimonious brother, who had forgotten his material debt to Tuco.

The sanctifying aura given to civilisation in the American Western has no place in the Italian Western which is more aware of its venality and oppression. It is the railroad capitalism of Morton (Gabriele Ferzetti) which results in the massacre of

the McBain family. When John Philip Law pursues the murderers of his family in *Death Rides a Horse* he finds several of them occupying positions of prominence in the new civilisation of the West. Wolcott (Luigi Pistilli) is a prominent politician, for one. In *The Big Gundown* this is the force which employs Corbett to pursue the innocent outcast Cucillo, in *Navajo Joe* it is the destroyer of the way of life of the Indians through the scalphunters, a force which it tolerates to its cost. Only in Giorgio Stegani's *Beyond the Law* is the aspect of civilisation viewed in a positive sense, but this is due to its conscious imitation of the

Luigi Pistilli in *Death Rides a Horse*.

is also threatened by the violent chaos of the Old West. Indio wipes out the family of the man who put him in jail in *For a Few Dollars More,* while in *Vengeance is Mine* the wife and child who would have integrated John Warner (George Hilton) away from the destructive path he is later to follow, perish through the prejudice of Sandoval (Ernest Borgnine). This is certainly not the picture of the family that we are accustomed to from the films of John Ford and most American directors. Far from being a revered, sanctified unit, it is shown to be weak and open to the dangers of the violent era of the Italian Western depiction. The classic example of the vulnerability of the family unit is seen in *A Fistful of Dollars* where Marisol (Marianne Koch) won at cards by Ramon (Gian-Maria Volonté). Husband and infant son live a humiliating existence outside the Rojo's house where they are often beaten up. It is the outsider No-Name who restores the unity of the family but only for his own reasons in breaking up the Rojos.

The whole area of the Italian Western is thus a complex one. We cannot possibly hope to examine every film in this field. Of the whole product comparatively few have been released here or in the States and what was released was out of the desire of distributors to cash in on a trend. Now Italy is making very few Westerns and is instead cashing in on the Kung-Fu craze, even adapting the Western to it. Two such examples are *Hercules versus Kung-Fu* scripted by Sergio Donati and Luciano Vincenzoni, and *To Kill or to Die.* Even the films released in this country have suffered. The thirty-five millimetre version of *The Good, the Bad and the Ugly* has almost twenty-five minutes cut from it while twenty minutes of key scenes are missing from *Once Upon a Time in the West.* Cuts have been made either out of the censor's squeamishness or the desire of the distributor to prune a main feature into a second feature. This not only ruins the integral pattern of each film, but also affects the continuity in a drastic way so that the

American Western with Lee Van Cleef riding a white horse in contrast to the black garbed figure of Gordon Mitchell riding a dark horse. In *Drop Them or I'll Shoot* the town is responsible for the death of Johnny Hallyday's innocent brother and has no redeeming features. Consequently the townspeople are humiliated by being stripped naked and made to lie flat on the street by the hippies, figures whom Corbucci clearly despises.

When it conflicts with the progress of civilisation the family unit is doomed as was the case with the McBains in *Once Upon a Time in the West.* But at the same time it

46

From *Drop Them or I'll Shoot.*

audience blames the director for the faults of the censor or distributor. Corbucci's *Django,* an important key work, has been banned here. It only slipped past the censor in a one-minute extract in the Jamaican film *The Harder They Come,* which was enough to make one appreciate the surrealistic colours utilised by Enzo Barboni. Sollima's *The Big Gundown* has been savagely mutilated by cuts which make the story line almost incomprehensible. Other key works still unreleased here include Corbucci's *The Grand Silence* with Jean-Louis Trintignant as a mute gunfighter pursuing his quarry in the snowy desert of North America, the third part of Sollima's political trilogy *Run Man Run,* and Colizzi's comic Western *Boot Hill. A Bullet for the General* has been cut to eighty-eight minutes, from its original running time of over two hours and the complete version of *Once Upon a Time in the West* still awaits release in this country.

The Italian Western was thus part of the Roman entertainment industry in the sixties. It will be our task to investigate the importance of the genre. The introductory comments we have made will serve as a background to the ensuing discussion; but one thing is certain: the genre is essentially a popular one as opposed to an intellectual art form. If Mann and Boetticher now belong to the intelligentsia, it is sobering to remind ourselves that such an audience was far from their minds when they were making Westerns. They were working in an essentially commercial concern in which success was measured by whether or not their films broke even at the box office. Like Leone much later, they judged their success as directors on general appeal to an audience, not to a minority of critics. It is interesting to read the reviews of some of their films when they first came out, as they too had their share of adverse criticism. It was not until a later time that their interests in the field of the Western were thoroughly understood. Who can claim that the same thing will not happen with the Italian Western?

Techniques, Motifs, and Directors

'He Said No to Chato!' (note attached to hanging body in *Find a Place To Die*)

The Italian Western differs from the American Western, mainly in its increased emphasis on the visuals and soundtrack, to enforce the emotional panorama of the film; this is in contrast to the usual narrative and dialogue structure of the traditional Western. One of the prime techniques is that of the *gundown*. In the Dollar Trilogy, tension is built up by concentration of the camera upon the faces and eyes of the protagonists. This is designed to show the

Mexicans and Gringos in *Django Kill!*

contrast between the initial confidence of the villain, and his later uncertainty as he begins to doubt his own powers. Relevant examples of this technique can be seen in the characters of Ramon (Gian-Maria Volonté in *A Fistful of Dollars*), Indio (Volonté in *For a Few Dollars More*) and Tuco (Eli Wallach) and Angel Eyes (Lee Van Cleef) in *The Good, the Bad and the Ugly*, with the emphatic devices of the musical score and rapid editing between the eyes, faces, holsters and long-shots of the main protagonists before the shoot-out begins.

These all serve to emphasise the conflict without the use of dialogue.

This use of visuals is not only limited to the gundown. In *Blindman* there is a striking scene where fifty white-gowned women run across a sandy desert, pursued on horseback by Mexican bandits against the background of blue cloudless sky, to the accompaniment of a rousing Cipriani score. This shows the almost surrealistic unearthly visual panorama which the Italian Western can be capable of. In the most surrealistic of Westerns, Giulio Questi's *Django · Kill!*,

Giuliano Gemma in *A Pistol for Ringo*.

Tomas Milian's mind flits back to the circumstances of his attempted murder by his 'gringo' fellow outlaws in fragmented imagery involving a rapidly fast montage of visuals and soundtrack. Again these are more important than actual dialogue in illustrating the mood and action of the film, and are thus foreign to hostile critics brought up in an opposing tradition.

The effect depends on the competence of the director concerned. Many wish only to imitate the American Western, but some like Carlo Lizzani wish to utilise the American tradition in their own way. In *The Hills Run Red* (1966), Lizzani utilises key figures of the American Westerns of Mann and Boetticher, Dan Duryea and Henry Silva (the last in a virtuoso extrovert performance) in an Americanised vendetta Western; while the Ringo films of Duccio Tessari use the themes of the American Western in a more interesting manner. A rare enthusiastic *Monthly Film Bulletin Review* may be quoted in regard to *A Pistol for Ringo* (1965).

Lovingly culled from a variety of sources ranging from Ford and Hawks to Raoul Walsh, this amalgam of well-tried Western situations is put together with real flair and sophistication. The action never lets up for a moment, the characters are vividly drawn, and the general line reminds one, oddly enough, of minor league Buñuel: not only in the gleeful cruelty of the Russian roulette variations invented by the bandit chief for selecting his daily victims, but also in the almost surrealistic contrast between the sweaty bandits and their aristocratically refined hosts. While murder and rapine flourish around her, for instance the heroine still finds time to instruct the major-domo to 'keep an eye on the souffle for me'; the sudden appearance of Dolores at the dinner table in a magnificent evening gown, with the Major in courtly attendance, is as startling as the sudden apparition by Signoret in the jungle in *La Mort en ce Jardin*; and at the end when the weaponless Ringo is held at bay the Major disappears in search of 'an old family heirloom that might be useful' and reappears with an ancient blunderbuss, casually muttering, 'This is the gun my grandfather fought with at Waterloo'. Though this kind of sidelong humour is the film's main weapon, it also scores heavily by observing the violent rules of the western genre: as Ringo himself remarks quoting an old Texan saying: 'God created men equal; the six-gun made 'em different'.

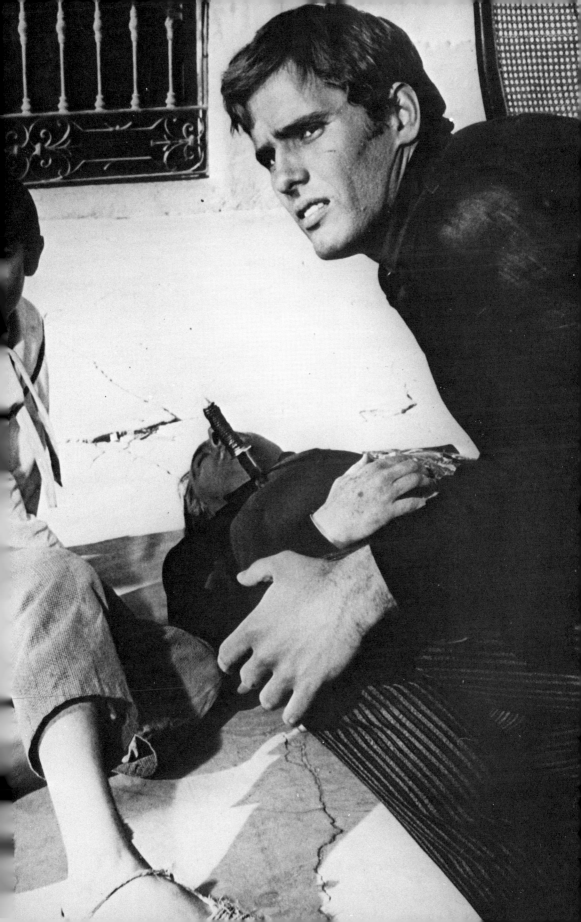

52

This also shows Tessari's use of satire in the genre. In the same year he made one of the best of the non-Leone Westerns, *The Return of Ringo,* using the same cast of matinée idol Giuliano Gemma, definitive Italian Western villain Fernando Sancho, Nieves Navarro and Antonio Casas in similar roles. This film is important because as well as using the old Western theme of a family being re-united against all odds Ringo has to discover his own identity in the course of the film. He begins by wearing the Union uniform but divests it for the anonymity of an outcast when he finds that Mexicans have not only taken over his town but also his wife. Normally Gemma is clean-

The return from *The Return of Ringo*.

Fernando Sancho in *Minnesota Clay*.

shaven in his matinée idol Italian Western roles, but this is the only time he appears with the inconographical beard and shabby clothes of the outsider, until he returns to his full identity at the close of the film. In most of his films Gemma has starred with a rep' company of actors such as Antonio Casas, Roberto Camardiel and Nello Pazzafini, usually confronting the villainous Fernando Sancho. Gemma's *Adios Gringo* (1965), was one unfortunate example of his matinée idol image being put to wrong use by an inappropriate director, which ended in absurdity. Comedy Westerns are normally uneven in the genre but *Seven Guns for the McGregors* (1965), **which Tessari co-scripted**

The bull-ring sequence in *Vengeance is Mine*.

and the Trinity Westerns of E. B. Clucher (Enzo Barboni), have been the most successful when the threat of overindulgence has been kept in check. There are borderlines in any division, and *Five Man Army* is one of them. Directed in 1965 by Don Taylor, from a story co-written by Dario Argento, it was more of a Western version of *Mission Impossible,* using the well-worn theme of stealing gold to aid the revolution. The Dutchman Peter Graves' was the most in-

congruous element, within a cast comprising key figures Bud Spencer and Nino Castelnuovo, which shows that even the presence of American actors in these Westerns cannot save the film in the hands of the wrong director. Franco Giraldi's appalling *Dead or Alive* with Alex Cord, Robert Ryan and Arthur Kennedy is one such example.

Many directors have made Westerns, which if not up to Leone's standards, have

Roberto Camardid and 'muchachos' in *Django Kill!*

been of interest. *Vengeance is Mine* (1969) directed by Julio Buchs, was a half-successful attempt depicting the corruption of victimised hero George Hilton by society, represented particularly by Ernest Borgnine who has a pathological hatred of 'gringos'. At its climax, the film expressed Hilton's conflict against society with him and his three outlaw gang trapped in the middle of a bullring and facing a gundown with the whole Mexican army. Not until *My Name is* *Nobody* (1973), was Leone to better that. Giulio Questi's single Western *Django Kill!* was a masterpiece of surrealism. Django, Tomas Milian, attempts to survive in the most corrupted town ever depicted in a Western, which thinks nothing of lynching a grotesque outlaw gang, in contrast to most Westerns where the latter normally terrorise the former. Django survives the attentions of perverted rancher Roberto Camardiel with his 'muchachos' and a

From *Today It's Me . . . Tomorrow You!*

religious fanatic storekeeper, and the film builds up to an apocalyptic climax of fire and dynamite with an ending anticipating the contamination of the children of the next generation as denoted in *The Wild Bunch*. Giulio Petroni was one of the few directors, apart from Leone, to use fully the talents of Lee Van Cleef in his competent revenge Western *Death Rides a Horse* (1967). His other films have included the political Western *Tepepa* (1968) which he co-scripted with Franco Solinas starring Tomas Milian and Orson Welles in a paradoxical tale of the revolutionary mythical hero, as exemplified by Milian. His other notable films have been *Night of the Snakes* (1969), *A Sky Full of Stars for a Roof* (1970) and *Life's Tough Eh, Providence,* with Tomas Milian as a lazy bounty hunter who travels the West in a carriage full of the latest labour saving devices for his job. *Today It's Me – Tomorrow You!* was an effective revenge Western directed by Tonino Cervi where Brett Halsey recruits five men, among whom are key genre character actors Bud Spencer, Wayde Preston and William Berger, to hunt down Samurai sword-wielding 'Mexican' Tatsuya Nakadai who murdered his wife and framed him. Unlike the American Western there is only one end – the death of the villain. Giuseppe Colizzi is one of the entertainment directors of the genre. His first Western *Blood River* (1967) was the beginning of a trilogy of films starring Terence Hill as Cat and Bud Spencer as Hutch; this was to anticipate their co-starring roles in the Trinity Westerns of E. B. Clucher. *Revenge at El Paso* (1968) was a much better Western than its uneven predecessor, having the advantage of Eli Wallach as Cacopoulos pursuing a vendetta against Kevin McCarthy. The film's highlight is a satire on the Leone gundown. It occurs in a gambling saloon, with an orchestra present which is made to play a waltz by Wallach, as accompaniment to the gundown – a mood which he has been dreaming of all those years in jail. This is a change from the usual trumpet theme. *Boot Hill* (1969) was set in a circus, taking

Colizzi's baroque interests to their utmost conclusion and having the advantage of Woody Strode, Lionel Stander and Victor Buono in the cast. Mario Lanfranchi's *Death Sentence* (1968) was a rather mediocre Revenge Western, but it had the advantage of two baroque cameos by Adolfo Celi and Tomas Milian. The former played a heavy, dressed as a minister of religion, with his gang garbed as deacons, preaching hellfire and damnation to his victims while torturing them for information. Milian mean-

while, forsook his scruffy Mexican persona of the genre, to portray a white-suited, neurotically sensitive, albino · epileptic, liable to go into seizure at the sight of a blonde or gold!

There have been a number of bad works in this field as there are in any genre. The 'Stranger' Westerns of Tony Anthony — *For a Dollar in the Teeth* (1966) and *Shoot First, Laugh Last!* (1967), both directed by Luigi Vanzi — have been little more than grotesque imitations of Leone's first two Westerns. Frank Kramer's *Sabata* (1969), despite having the presence of Lee Van Cleef, was merely a mixture of gimmickry and borrowed themes which were to be repeated *ad nauseum* in his other Westerns — *The Bounty Hunters* (1970) and *The Return of Sabata* (1971). However the presence of the bad works only serves to throw into relief the innovations made by the true artists of the genre and to them we now turn.

Lee van Cleef and friend pay an offset homage to Luis Buñuel during the filming of *Sabata*.

Sergio Leone

Harmonica: 'So you found out you're not a businessman after all'.
Frank: 'Just a man'.
Harmonica: 'An ancient race'.

Cheyenne: 'People like that have something inside – something to do with death'. (from *Once Upon a Time in the West*).

Without doubt Sergio Leone is the most important director in the Italian Western field, perhaps in the whole genre of the Western. More than anyone else he has extended the previously fixed limits of the Western to new horizons, so that the old boundaries of narrative and realism have expanded into a mythic-poetic vision, based upon an intelligent combination of visuals and soundtrack. Before he made *A Fistful of Dollars* in 1964, he had already acquired experience in the technical expertise of film-making both in his own country and in combination with directors such as Walsh, Wise, Wyler and Zinneman. After directing two epic films – *The Last Days of Pompeii* and *Colossus of Rhodes* (1960) and co-directing *Sodom and Gomorrah* (1962) with Robert Aldrich, he bowed out of film-making until he managed to raise finance for a Western which he decided to treat with a 'cold, European irony'. Though the plot was merely a re-working of Kurosawa's *Yojimbo* Leone has claimed that

The 'Iconographic Stranger'; Eastwood in *The Good, the Bad and the Ugly*.

his real inspiration was Goldoni's play *Harlequin, the Servant of Two Masters*. Kurosawa is an admirer of John Ford and the *Yojimbo* score is a Westernised one, so that Leone's treatment of the subject differed a lot from Kurosawa's, as will be shown. This was the film which launched the boom in Italy, having grossed nearly eight million dollars though budgeted for less than $80,000.

The opening of a Leone Western is always of fundamental importance, especially in upsetting the established conventions of the genre. After the blinding sun hails the end of the credits in *A Fistful of Dollars,* as it 'does in the rest of the Dollar Trilogy, the scene focuses on a poncho-garbed man riding a mule. We are familiar with the scene from countless American Westerns but not the details. As he draws water from the well we see that he is no Mexican, as the poncho would have led us to suppose, but a 'gringo', the 'hero' of the film. This introductory shot is important as it shows the contradictory nature of No-Name – the main figure of Leone's first trilogy. He is the cinematic stranger answering to no particular name whether it be Joe, Il Monko, or Blondie. Normally he is a bounty hunter, a profession despised by the community and outlaws alike. He has no fixed origin, his clothes betray his lack of identity. At the beginning of the film he enters a community to which he does not belong, and at the climax he has left it in ruins with a trail of corpses in his wake. By appearance he contradicts the usual clean-cut image of the Western hero: he is untidy, wears a poncho which is normally the trade-mark of the type-cast Mexican in the American Western, and rides not a horse but a mule. Already in this opening shot Leone has upset the Western conventions radically.

In the rest of the film he continues his usurpation of the conventions by conducting his film with elements of black humour, increased use of violence, and the prominent use of the Morricone score, most notably in the gundown. Two important elements stand out. First, the figure of the outsider with no connections exemplified in the non-categorical figure of Eastwood is established, free from the ties and laws of the community. Secondly, the weakness of the family unit is shown in the figure of Marisol forced to be Ramon's mistress. In Leone's early films the figure of the woman is always an insecure one. She is either a good lay to the hero/villain or a prey to rape and murder. In Leone's vision of the brutal era of the Old West the woman never has a clearly-defined personality of her own. Not until *Once Upon a Time in the West* will a different picture emerge.

A Fistful of Dollars is clearly an apprentice work; the themes are there but they have yet to be fully developed. *For a Few Dollars More* is the most refined of the mid-sixties Italian Westerns and sets the standard by which the majority should be judged. Here No-Name in contrast to the previous film has a defined profession – the despised pursuit of bounty hunter. His sole aim is the acquisition of gold, the only aim worthy of achievement in the West. That may have been the aim in *A Fistful of Dollars* but it seems to have been neglected in the latter part of the film when the course is directed towards the revenge on Ramon. Gian-Maria Volonté appeared once more under his real name playing Indio, a drug-crazed psychotic killer; while the second lead, Colonel Mortimer, was played by a notable American actor, Lee Van Cleef. Though he had worked in the States under directors such as Ford, Mann and Boetticher he had never been given full opportunity to display his excellent talents at characterisation until Leone. Even critics of the film grudgingly acclaimed Van Cleef's performance. Not only did this film see the beginning of Leone's interest in the alliance between men of different generations, but it also showed the interrelationships amongst the three participants which made up the course of the film – No-Name, Indio and Mortimer.

The opening of the film which introduces these three men is similar to that in *The Good, the Bad and the Ugly*. It is particularly important in the depiction of Mortimer.

What is of interest in the beginning is the appearance of the train, for two reasons: it shows the beginning of civilisation reaching the still untamed West, in contrast to the quiet Mexican town of the first film where the action had occurred; and secondly, it shows the germ of interest in the railroad which will reach its highest expression in *Once Upon a Time in the West*. When No-Name seeks information about Mortimer from the Prophet (Josef Egger) he ascribes both his and Mortimer's seeming decline to the development of the railroad. It is already a sign of the changing times.

After this shot we have a close-up of a Bible in front of a man's face. When the guard approaches the Bible is lowered to reveal the thin hawk-like features of a man in his late forties who stops the train prematurely at the destination he wants. The man's revolver suddenly pointing at the conductor puts a stop to any objections. He is either a lawman or a bounty hunter. When he enquires about the poster of a wanted man at the station, we know it is the latter profession. At the town his pursuit of his quarry is calm, unhurried and methodical, aided by his arsenal of period rifles rolled up in his saddle-bags. Up to now we have not seen the face of his quarry. When he has shot the horse from under his fleeing

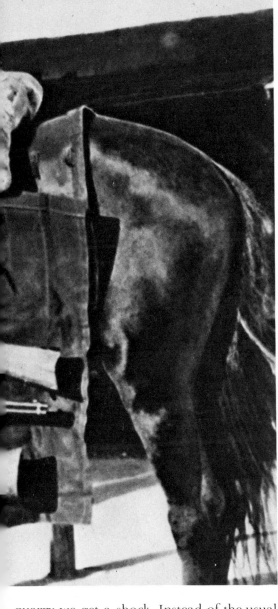

Mortimer in *For a Few Dollars More*.

men, and appears as a demonic psychotic killer. Thus the order which will be present in the other Westerns is now revealed with protagonist and protagonist against a third party. In the next film No-Name and Tuco have an unstable alliance against Angel Eyes, while Cheyenne and Harmonica ally against Frank in *Once Upon a Time in the West*.

As to the motives of the two bounty hunters in pursuing Indio, Leone depicts these in an original manner. No-Name's glance focuses on the reward money on a wanted poster, while Mortimer's concentrates on the words 'Dead or Alive'. Gunshots echo on the soundtrack between cuts of Indio's face on the reward poster and those words, so we know which alternative is meant. His motives are essentially personal. This will not be the last time that Leone will give us a visual clue in his films (cf. the position of the model railway engine in the frame during the dialogue between Jill and Cheyenne in *Once Upon a Time in the West*).

As in the former film the elements of black comedy, violence and prominent use of the score again occur. Other features are present. When No-Name and Mortimer first meet they have a childish encounter and both first stub each other's toes. One of the audience of small Mexican boys watching this sees the parallel with the games they themselves play and this is reminiscent of Silvanito's comment in *A Fistful of Dollars* – 'It's like playing cowboys and Indians' – while spying on Ramon's activities. No doubt this is intentional as Leone wishes to show that the ritual of confrontation is in many cases no different from a children's game. Their games may be seen as training into adulthood when there is no playing for dead. Indio's psychotic tendencies take a novel form. After ordering the slaughter of his betrayer's family he challenges him to a gunfight to the accompaniment of a musical watch. This is his fetish by which he relives a past experience under drugs when he had murdered a young man and raped his wife.

quarry we get a shock. Instead of the usual handsome second lead we are so accustomed to from conventional Westerns, the face is that of an actual degenerate which bears no relation to his wanted poster. Thus Leone has mocked another well-worn cliché. After felling him with a long-distance rifle, Mortimer finishes the job with a short-distance one. This is the first vignette denoting one main character, whose professionalism as a bounty hunter is well attested, and is in contrast to the next scene showing the rough and ready methods which No-Name uses, leaving full scope for any unforeseen circumstances. The third scene reveals Indio to us. He is sprung from jail by his

66

The key to that scene has been cut out by the censor. Though we know that the woman was Mortimer's sister, in a later version of this, we see that she had committed suicide with Indio's gun while being raped by him. This is undoubtedly the reason for his psychosis as by listening to the watch he existentially relives his pathological sex-death obsession at each confrontation. Indio's murder of the family is carried out in a deserted Church, and is depicted with the aid of Morricone's organ and trumpet combination in the score, giving it the intensity of an ecstatic mock Catholic mass. Indio's killings clearly have a religious dimension for him. Leone reinforces this imagery later, when Indio preaches his gang a sermon from the pulpit – the parable of the Carpenter – while his disreputable gang listen like a faithful flock to its parson. It must not be forgotten also that when Luigi Pistilli and his men arrive at the Church they announce themselves by shooting at the bell. If religion is defunct in this world the feelings which have given rise to it are channelled in other directions.

The other great feature of the film is, of course, the development of the gundown. When the final confrontation occurs between Mortimer and Indio, No-Name supervises it with Mortimer's watch running (a similar one to Indio's) to ensure fair play. With three men present we have the genesis of the triple gundown. To the accompaniment of a Morricone score, it is not the draw which is important but the emotional build-up to it. The settling of a vendetta is an intensely personal affair and the use of visuals and soundtrack emphasises this. Once Indio dies the vendetta is complete and the men of different generations part, Mortimer giving his share to No-Name, so dissolving the partnership. The film's closing shot is a cynical one of No-Name riding a wagon filled with the bodies of Indio and his gang. Death definitely has its price as their lives were of no value.

Due to its increased budget, *The Good, the Bad and the Ugly* represents an advance upon the format of Leone's first two Westerns in scope. Here he attempts to create an epic Western, again reflecting his personal vision of the Old West, but this time against a clearly defined historical setting. His previous experience in the field of Italian spectaculars, and also his work with major American directors, provided the right combination of crowd control scenes of an epic nature, together with an outlook which would appeal to an international audience. *The Good, the Bad and the Ugly* pushes the genre to the highest limits imaginable both in theme and spectacle, succeeding amply in both spheres. Leone has been quoted as saying, that the day American screenwriters discover the inexhaustible wealth of story and screen material the United States has to offer, Italy's film industry will be unemployed. This film, along with his undisputed masterpiece *Once Upon a Time in the West*, illustrates his mastery in the field of genre

Above, below and previous page: Leone as historian from *The Good, the Bad and the Ugly.*

extension. As well as being a director who can present material professionally to a popular audience, Leone is also an able historian for the period of his films. The Civil War episodes of the prison camp and the battle of the bridge, bear a striking resemblance to the Civil War photographs of Matthew Brady which is not surprising since Leone shot many of the scenes with the actual period photos on his lap, and can safely claim that his film is more accurate than any American Western on that score.

Despite the Civil War occupying only a minor proportion of the film, it is still the epochal event within it. No-Name, Tuco and Angel Eyes move across a tormented West caught in the throes of the conflict. Armies advance and retreat, many of the towns are either being shelled or are already devastated by cannon. Examples of the mutilated are seen, such as Half-Soldier whose only function is to spy for Angel-Eyes. The legless Commandant of the

'Half-soldier' from *The Good, the Bad and the Ugly.*

munity are involved as opposed to the outsiders, the bounty hunter No-Name, Mexican outcast Tuco and professional killer Angel Eyes. The conventional distinction of 'good', 'bad', and 'ugly' does not apply to each character as they are themselves a mixture of these qualities. They are a creation of the morality of the landscape which they occupy and abide by its rules. Their purpose is at least positive, as opposed to the aimless Civil War slaughter. It is the search for Civil War bullion which is their motivation. The three start from separate points in the framework of the film, and encounter each other at the climax in the now classic gundown. They cynically don the uniforms of the opposing sides whenever it suits their purpose. While No-Name and Tuco don Southern colours, Angel Eyes infiltrates a Union prison camp, to await the man who knows the location of the gold among the remnants of the defeated South. While the opposing armies are either occupied in shooting deserters, evacuating towns, strapping spies to the front of trains as examples, the Trio work positively by any means at their disposal to gain the gold. For whichever side wins, the rich will be the victors. The only victims of the conflict are the conscientious Union captain – who can only get drunk before leading his men in a futile charge across a bridge; the young soldier whom No-Name finds dying in agony at the other side; and the various mutilated soldiers seen throughout the film.

With the excellent photography of Tonino Delli Colli replacing Massimo Dallamano, the film introduces three protagonists to us in separate vignettes, similar to *For a Few Dollars More.* After the conventional sun motif of the Trilogy the film opens to a landscape which is suddenly filled with the weather-worn face of Al Mulock. Other figures are seen in the distance getting off their horses and approaching him. Our first thought is of a classic confrontation between three men. This is nullified when the three, obviously

Union prison camp is powerless to act against the terrorism of Angel Eyes, and the wounded find temporary shelter in the monastery of Father Ramirez. As opposed to the majority of the American directors, Leone has an individual treatment of the theme. Whereas the Civil War is usually depicted as a heroic chapter in the formation of the *United States* of America or simply as mere melodramatic background, Leone sees the whole event as futile and aimless. It is a pursuit in which the com-

Futility of war from *The Good, the Bad and the Ugly*.

there by some kind of agreement suddenly halt by the door of a saloon and charge in. Shots ring out, and a Mexican with a joint of meat in his hand jumps through a window and is held in freeze frame while the words 'Il Bruto' (The Ugly) fill the screen. He then escapes on horseback before Mulock, the only survivor of the three, can attempt a shot at him. As Tuco, Eli Wallach seems at first the cinematic Mexican – scruffy, dissolute and immoral – but we are later to find out he is a man of character forced to become an outlaw by circumstances. With an excellent character-isation, combining full-blooded humour with treacherous and avaricious traits, Wallach's performance is the highlight of the film, which owes much to Leone's direction. His bandit role in *Magnificent Seven* differs from Tuco in that where he seems to be a method actor playing at being a Mexican in the former film, here Leone makes us believe in his character absolutely. Similar vignettes introduce Angel Eyes and No-Name. The former is a cold-blooded killer, portrayed excellently by Lee Van Cleef, who massacres two-thirds of a family after helping himself to their table and pursuing his ruthless ethic of completing the job, no matter who pays him, to its utmost conclusion. No-Name is again Eastwood who does not don his iconographical guise until the close of the film. One of the virtues of Leone in this film is that he pairs him with Wallach, in a semi-comic relationship with the macabre undertones of best black comedy.

As well as the usual elements of violence and black comedy which mark Leone's work, we have the similar themes of family unit insecurity, and the helplessness of the woman exemplified by the figures of Chelo Alonso and Rada Rassimov (the last subjected to a brutal beating by Angel Eyes for Bill Carson's whereabouts). One of the most ironic sequences occurs in the Union prisoner of war camp, which Angel Eyes runs on lines no different to a concentration camp. Tuco is invited to a meal by Angel Eyes and is subjected to a

Angel eyes' from *The Good, the Bad and the Ugly.*

Above and opposite: Women as victims from *The Good the Bad and the Ugly.*

At the station from *Once Upon a Time in the West*.

brutal beating by Wallace (Mario Brega), breaking off only when the latter is about to gouge his eyes out. While this is going on, an orchestra of Confederates is forced to play a musical accompaniment of 'The Story of a Soldier', a common occurrence in the camp. The Nazi parallel needs no pressing. In a deleted sequence a young soldier with one inflamed eye (a victim of Wallace?) breaks down while playing but is forced to continue by a brutal guard. Another important scene is that of No-Name encountering the dying young Confederate boy. He covers him with his coat and offers him a cigar out of sympathy. This shows us that he is no brutal existentialist, as some have held, but a man who can be sympathetic to the plight of others. Both he and the boy are victims of the world in which they live. No-Name survives in the way he can because it is the only way

for him in the West. He is not the victim of inexperience like the young soldier, nor is he tied to the vulnerable family unit. In the aftermath of the violent battle he says nothing, but can only offer a gesture of mutual solidarity in a world both he and the boy are powerless to change.

The climax of the film is of course, the triple gundown between the three protagonists, carrying the circular *corrida* motif to its highest expression. In no other Western are the existential limits of Leone's view of the gunfight as akin to a modern form of the ancient ritual combat in an ecstatic life-death metaphor so exemplified by the use of close-ups, rapid editing and Morricone score. When the three meet the gundown must occur conclusively, determining their destinies and their professionalism The scene occurs in a graveyard, probably of Civil War victims, and not only attests to the futility of the whole conflict but visually expresses the whole iconography of death, by which the Trilogy had been surrounded. Building up to an intense pitch after the best part of five minutes, the outcome is decided and with it the last appearance of No-Name in the Leone opus.

After the success of the Trilogy, Leone was offered complete freedom by Paramount to make another Western, so he chose to make a completely different product from his other films, expressing a unique personal vision. This was his masterpiece to which Leone contributed on the script with Sergio Donati and Bernardo Bertolucci from a story co-written by himself, Bertolucci and Dario Argento – *Once Upon a Time in the West*. Misunderstood at the time of its release and cut in most countries by some twenty minutes, it is the climatic expression of romanticism in the Italian Western vision.

At the opening of the film three men arrive at a train depot in the middle of a desert, empty except for the aged ticket collector and an Indian woman – only the sound of a creaking windmill breaks the silence. One is instantly recognisable as Jack Elam, character actor from countless American Westerns, the second is Woody Strode, John Ford's Sergeant Rutledge, while the third is Leone's own Al Mulock. No word is spoken by these men, obviously not men to be trifled with. Elam disdainfully looks at the old man's offer of railway tickets, leads him forcefully into a cupboard gesturing him to be silent. The Indian woman runs away cursing in the distance. Thus the three wait as the credits roll. The five minutes which elapse until the train arrives are among the most masterfully conceived in the cinema. With no dialogue, the camera scrupulously observes the actions of the three, so that we virtually know all there is to know about them. Elam is slouching on a chair, tearing out the wires of the telegraph machine to stop the noisy clatter, a fly buzzes 'irritatingly' about him, he catches it in the barrel of his gun and listens to it in contentment; Mulock cracking his knuckles, and Strode, impassive as water-drops sprinkle on the brim of his hat from the water turret. The scene is an obvious parody of *High Noon* which expresses Leone's deliberate but masterful control of mood within the film, in opposition to the gross violence and gimmickry of most Italian Westerns. It also expresses his contempt for the American Western's 'guest star' system, as his three 'stars' here are to be immediately obliterated by Harmonica. They are *actors* not stars in Leone's view. His visual depiction of Jack Elam gives us more cinematic detail and characterisation of that actor than his twenty or so years in the American cinema. Thus a third factor is that here we have a subtle pointer into how to get the best characterisation out of one's actors. This opening scene has one of the most accomplished usages of the wide screen with its spatial imagery than ever used before in a Western.

As the film's title suggests, the story looks back at the Old West in the manner of a fairy tale. For Leone, the world of the Italian Western is quickly fading and its era becoming a fond reminiscence. Gone are No-Name, Colonel Mortimer, Tuco. In their place has arisen the development of civilisation. This is depicted in the drive across Monument Valley by Sam and Jill. When Jill (Claudia Cardinale) alights at the station at Flagstone the camera cranes up as she speaks to the inspector to show the emergent new life of the developing town. We have already seen other passengers at the station and here Leone's background detail should be noted. The passengers include diverse personalities. Easterners, a young boy with tuberculosis in a wheelchair, and most significantly, Indians who are travelling in undignified fashion in the cattle-truck part of the train. All Leone's Westerns are realistic in manner in so far as they show authentic background locations, sweaty, unshaven people typical of the time. Yet here we have the beginning of a new era in the West. The Monument Valley sequence is no parody but a sign of the changing times. Railway lines are

The helplessness of women from *Today It's Me . . . Tomorrow You!*

being laid, a fact which disgusts Jill's driver Sam (Paolo Stoppa). For Leone, it was clearly not enough to film this scene just anywhere, for he wishes to make clear that the whole West is in process of change, not the Italian West. So what better location could best exemplify it than Monument Valley?

It is no accident that the film's main character is a woman, since Leone suggests that the West is now becoming safe for the woman herself and with her, civilisation. Cheyenne and Harmonica both realise this in their way, as they do the most to prepare Jill for her new role. Previously as a prostitute, she was like them, an outcast figure. Now she is soon to be part of a new society, which is developing in the West with the arrival of the railroad.

An interest in the Irish immigrant role in the formation of America is seen by Leone here. An expatriate Irishman destroys Juan's innocence in *A Fistful of Dynamite* and the element will figure prominently in Leone's forthcoming *Once Upon a Time – America*. It is Frank and his gang who accomplish the deed. When all the McBains have been killed except for one small boy, who stands silently in the porch, several figures in dusters emerge in long-shot from the scrub and approach the house. As they near the boy, Leone has one of his cinematic shock effects as the camera circles from the back of the leader straight into his face, close-up. It is that of Henry Fonda, the traditional good guy of countless American Westerns, here demonically transformed into a thoroughly evil character. Since one of his gang has called him by name, he kills the boy, smiling as he does so.

A director who can make us believe in Henry Fonda as a credible villain in spite of all the films he has made in the opposite mould (Wyatt Earp in *My Darling Clementine*, or the title role in *Young Mr Lincoln* for example) is worthy of the highest recognition. Fonda's characterisation is thoroughly believable, fitting in as it does with the Leone view of the main protagonist. There are three such figures in the film, the first of

Cardinale and Fonda from *Once Upon a Time in the West*.

which is Frank. He is the representative of the vicious killer of the Old West whose sadistic tendencies are now at the disposal of railroad capitalist Morton (Gabriele Ferzetti) who is out to destroy the Old West, the heritage from which Frank arose. His power of the gun is soon becoming limited as Morton possesses the greater power, that of money, which he later uses to pay Frank's own gang to kill him. Frank believes himself to be part of the new order of capitalism but he soon realises that he is just a man, an ancient race. His efforts are as futile as if he had attempted to marry Jill to gain Sweetwater, but there he is realistic enough to see that he would be 'no good as a husband'. After the course of events have defeated him, he has to return to solve the enigma of Harmonica. . . As he says to Harmonica: 'It wouldn't have bothered Morton knowing you were around somewhere', so stating his essential incom-

patibility with the Mortons, the new men of the West. He has to face Harmonica thus sealing his essential identity with the world of the Old West which is now passing. His brand of vicious lawlessness is now anachronistic, as Morton had remarked.

Like Frank, Cheyenne (Jason Robards) represents an era of lawlessness out of tune with the new West. Like Frank, he has his gang who loyally obey his commands, but do so up to the end. He represents the old style, almost folk-heroic amoral type of outlaw who is a dying breed. At the beginning of the film he can still run rings round any posse but gradually the forces of civilisation are limiting his freedom. He has something in common with Jill – his mother was 'the biggest whore in Alameda and the finest woman anywhere' who must have made his father of a few hours or days a very happy man. But if Jill begins from the position of outsider in the community, she soon finds her place – a place gently urged upon her by Cheyenne in many ways, most notably in bringing the needs of the railroad construction gang to her attention at the close of the film. At his first meeting the city-bred Jill was unaccustomed to making coffee. When he next meets her she has already mastered this simple task of the frontierswoman. While she serves the new cosmopolitan nation of America at the film's climax, he is already dying as he rides away with Harmonica. It is his death which is the real conclusion of the film; a conclusion which sums up the real irony of the title. Just a short distance from the railway track he slumps from his saddle to the ground. Harmonica finds that he is dying of a bullet wound in the stomach inflicted by Morton, 'Mr Choo-Choo, who, leaves two shiny tracks just like a snail', when his gang had attacked the train to free him. Like Steve Judd in *Guns in the Afternoon* he wishes to die alone and Harmonica discreetly acknowledges his request standing with back turned as the slumped figure of Cheyenne collapses. Then both depart

unnoticed by the New America.

If Cheyenne dies at the film's climax Harmonica is already dead. His name determines his function; having no real personality, he is known only by the instrument he plays during the film. Leone uses the frozen immobility of the Charles Bronson persona to the best possible advantage. The instrument provides him with his sole purpose for existence. He is one of the walking dead of the Old West, answering only to the names of the men Frank had killed long ago. He might just as well have been his brother returned from the grave. Harmonica is the final extension of the Italian Western hero. Like No-Name he is outside society but whereas the former's aim was gold, Harmonica's is exclusively the fulfilment of a vendetta. No-Name's desire in *For a Few Dollars More* was to eventually become a rancher. Harmonica acquires McBain's dream of Sweetwater from Cheyenne's reward money but he bequeaths it to Jill. Whereas Colonel Mortimer can ride away purged of the unhappy cancer which has been

Leone and Cardinale during the filming of *Once Upon a Time in the West*.

festering inside him for years in *For a Few Dollars More*, Harmonica's purgation of his vendetta can have no such conclusion. It has provided him with his only means for living throughout the years. He really died when his brother did, as Leone depicts the young Bronson in the flashback, wearing the same clothes as the adult. Cheyenne wisely observes that despite Jill's hopes Harmonica will never settle down anywhere. He has 'something to do with death' which puts him on the other side of humanity. He rides off with a vague farewell of returning 'some day'. Thus in Leone's hands the liability which so many critics have commented upon in regard to Bronson becomes a virtue. It is two dead men who ride away at the film's climax.

We have already remarked on the importance of Jill's role, which is easily understandable against the background of Leone's other films. She begins as an outsider – the best whore in New Orleans – and ends as personifying the acceptable figure of the Matriarchy of the traditional Western. She committed the cardinal sin of any whore – marriage with a client – to participate in McBain's dream of Sweetwater which gives her a definable historical function within a community at the film's climax. As she remarks to Cheyenne, she would not have minded giving McBain half a dozen kids in return for the chance of doing *something* with herself. She is uncertain of this *something* but she is persuaded in different ways by Cheyenne and Harmonica to find it in Sweetwater instead of returning to the anonymity of New Orleans. Only when she is threatened by Frank does she revert back to her old role to save her life, a role which she cleanses herself of afterwards by a hot bath.

The film is also notable for having the last serious Leone gundown, this time with only Frank and Cheyenne as protagonists. Frank has returned to solve the enigma of Harmonica. To the opening of the best of Morricone's gundown score the confrontation begins. A sense of monumental fluidity is contributed to by the camerawork of Tonino Delli Colli, in the circular area

denoting the spheres of life and death in which the protagonists move. Unlike other Leone gundowns this one uses the flashback technique to solve the enigma of Harmonica's role for the audience's satisfaction and also to link the present conflict indissolubly with the incident which engendered it in the past. It is a technique which is not used in the gundown between Mortimer and Indio in *For a Few Dollars More*. At previous points of the film where Harmonica has encountered Frank we have seen the use of flashback in which

Coburn and Steiger in *A Fistful of Dynamite*.

a figure walks towards us in blurred-focus slow motion. The obscurity is now removed and we see that it is the Frank of many years past who has strung Harmonica's brother by the neck on a bell-rope from an arch. In the background is Monument Valley. Only Harmonica supports his brother on his shoulders while Frank sneeringly shoves a harmonica into his mouth until his brother curses Frank and kicks Harmonica away. The harmonica plays a similar role to that of Indio's watch. It is the symbol of a past event which determines a character's role throughout his life leading to his eventual confrontation with his opponent in the arena of life and death. As the camera wheels round Harmonica slowly at the beginning of the conflict then remains stationary for the period of the flashback, while both men are facing each other, the score and visual montage predominate until the decisive moment when Frank is shot and learns the answer to the enigma of Harmonica.

Thus with the beginning of the Matriarchy represented by Jill, the definitive world of the Italian Western ends. There is now no place for men like Frank, Cheyenne or Harmonica. The forces of law and order now have full power and it is notable that the figure of Keenan Wynn is one of the few honest and powerful sheriffs in the Italian Western. When Jill remains alone for Leone, the dream which he has been instrumental in creating has come to an end.

Anything after *Once Upon a Time in the West* would seem anti-climatic, especially *A Fistful of Dynamite* which is perhaps the most unsatisfactory of Leone's films. Like its predecessor it is not the Leone of the Dollar films but whereas Leone had carefully prepared the former (which seems to be his policy in all his films) he had originally only intended to produce it. Utilising again his theme of the interplay between men of different generations he originally wanted Jason Robards for the part of the Mexican bandit Juan, and Malcolm McDowall for the disillusioned ex-IRA idealist Sean. This would have resulted in a clearer dichotomy than that which emerged in the final film. However, since Steiger and Coburn had already been signed for the film and refused to appear unless Leone himself directed, to his annoyance Leone had no time for his usual careful pre-production work and had to adapt the film as he went along. Though the film is not a complete failure and has many interesting Leone insights it is overtly ponderous and takes an inordinate amount of time to develop its themes.

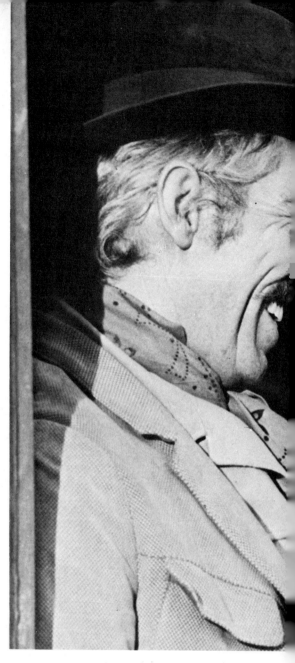

However, the merit of the film is in its deflation of another heroic myth of the cinema – the Revolution. Whereas the Revolution is usually seen in the American cinema as leading to a change for the better, in line with its usual use of cinematic historical inaccuracy as in *Juarez*, *Viva Zapata* and *Vera Cruz*, *A Fistful of Dynamite* reflects a much more accurately pessimistic view acting as a necessary antidote to those over-optimistic Latin American Third World films and the commercialised Italian political Westerns. The figure of the naïve inexperienced bandit Juan is set against that of the politically experienced yet naïvely idealistic Sean. It is Juan who is critical of revolutions organised by intellectuals of other classes that never bring the practical benefits to the people. After experiencing Juan's criticism of the myth of the Revolution it is Sean who throws away his copy of the anarchist writer Bakunin. This no doubt represents Leone's personal view, a view which is still relevant to contemporary society, pessimistically identifying Revolution with confusion as he has

Sean and Juan – political idealist and naive bandit.

himself pointed out. In *Once Upon a Time in the West* Leone had expressed his view of the West in romantic imagery. In *A Fistful of Dynamite* the theme of the Revolution is seen in terms of a nihilistic mythology. Sean's presence is announced by an explosion of dynamite when he appears on a vehicle of the twentieth century, the motorbike, which abruptly contrasts with the carriage of the previous scene. Juan sees the letters MESA VERDE form above Sean's head, with an image of gold, seeing in the latter an aid to the great wealth he has dreamt of, a belief he is to be abruptly robbed of later in the film. Mesa Verde itself, with the bank which Juan thinks both he and Sean are to rob, is depicted less in a realistic sense and more in terms of dream-like imagery. It is a foreign landscape dominated by the sound of the frequent executions, almost desolate, and subjugated by the posters of the tyrannical Don Jaimie (Franco Graziosi) depicted like a gigantic god dispensing material benefits to his people.

A Fistful of Dynamite is set in 1913, the

Sean in *A Fistful of Dynamite*.

same time as the majority of Italian political
Westerns and has the theme of the domination of the peasant by the gringo. In this
case Juan believes that Sean will lead him to
great wealth but is gradually brought into
the arena of the Revolution losing both
political innocence and bandit family in
the process until he accidentally ends up
as a revolutionary hero by killing Don
Jaimie. His old life is lost and the gesture
made by the dying Sean at the film's conclusion, of restoring Juan's rosary, which
Juan had thrown away at the death of his
family is far too late. At the film's final
scene Juan is left alone against the desolate
background of the night.

Sean is the absolute contrast to Juan.
He is an intellectual, a political, idealistic
dynamite expert wanted by the British for
his Irish revolutionary activities. Like
Harmonica he is a man haunted by death,
which in this case is symbolised by the
sticks of dynamite he carries with him, the
only reality which he believes in. He is a
man haunted by his past life in Ireland, by
visions of the pleasant times he used to
have with his best friend and their girl.
So as with other Leone figures such as

Harmonica, Colonel Mortimer and Indio
this memory of a past association is in-
eradicable and dominates their present
action. In Sean's case he had personally
killed his friend who had betrayed him
under torture, a failing which his idealistic
nature makes no allowance for. It is only
when he comes to realise that even the best
of men such as the revolutionary Dr Villega
(Romolo Valli) can crack under such
pressures that his final moral collapse
occurs. As a result he chooses to return
once more to his egoistical fantasy at the
close of the film choosing to be re-united
with it at death. By that time his damage to
the life of Juan is irreparable.

In common with the rest of his films, *A
Fistful of Dynamite* has the same mixture of
humour, violence and black comedy, and
favourite themes such as the interplay
between men of different generations. With
sombre photography by Giuseppe Ruzzolini
and idiosyncratic score by Morricone, it is
a personal work in the same way as
Peckinpah's equally flawed *Ballad of Cable
Hogue*. The beginning is marked by some
grotesque ·close-ups of bourgeois eating
like animals as they humiliate Juan in the

carriage, which expresses Juan's own view of them, a satire on the *corrida* motif which is the area where Juan rapes the repressed bourgeois wife, and comic interludes between Steiger and his family. The attack on the Mesa Verde bank where Juan frees imprisoned revolutionaries instead of the gold he has been expecting is one of the film's highlights. Thus, though flawed, *A Fistful of Dynamite* expresses an intense personal vision which is highly pessimistic, contributing to one of the cinema's main themes in a macabre mythical vein.

Though *A Fistful of Dynamite* is Leone's last completed film to date as a director before his long awaited gangster film *Once*

Terence Hill as Nobody in *My Name is Nobody*.

Upon a Time — America, he has left us with another indirect example of his legacy in the comedy western *My Name is Nobody.* That this film is vastly successful is due less to its director Tonino Valerii, but more to Leone as its producer bearing the same general relation to the Hawks-Nyby *Thing from Another World* in the influence of a lesser by a greater talent.

The film is a gentle send-up, not only of the second-generation Trinity, Italian Westerns but also of key elements of Leone's own Westerns. With Terence Hill identical to Trinity in all but name, it seems to be Leone's intention to show the comedy Western directors how to best utilise the comic elements of the genre properly, while at the same time mocking both themselves and his own conventions such as the gundown, close-ups and the opening ambushes of *The Good, the Bad and the Ugly* and *Once Upon a Time in the West.* Leone's dissatisfaction with the Trinity films was doubtless his reason for casting Terence Hill as Nobody, paying a fond farewell to the genre he was instrumental in creating but now usurped by the Trinity films. In a film where the humour and satire are predominant the story is of little consequence. Ageing gunfighter Jack Beauregard (Henry Fonda) wishes to retire from a West with which he now has little sympathy and sail away to Europe. The significance of this journey needs little emphasis here. However, Nobody wishes to see his idol reach the climax of his career by facing a gundown with one-hundred-and-fifty 'sons of bitches' – the Wild Bunch! How this is eventually realised occupies the plot of the film. At the opening Leone parodies not only the opening of his latter Westerns where Henry Fonda kills three outlaws attempting to ambush him with one bullet, but also the slow-motion balletic death so dear to Sam Peckinpah, a technique which occurs elsewhere in the film. Later when Jack meets Nobody (who like Harmonica answers only to the names of the men Jack has killed) in a graveyard the latter finds a tombstone with the unpro-

Terence Hill in *My Name is Nobody*.

nounceable name of 'Sam Peckinpah'!
It is at this graveyard, the significance of
which is apparent from *The Good, the Bad
and the Ugly,* that Jack attempts to force
Nobody into a gundown by shooting off
his hat several times, the same method
that No-Name uses with Colonel Mortimer
in *For a Few Dollars More*. With several
examples of the burlesque comedy routines
of the Trinity films, performed excellently
by Terence Hill, the film reaches its eventual
climax, when Jack becomes finally
fascinated with Nobody's dream and takes
on the Wild Bunch, a gang whose theme
is a masterly Morricone send up of the title
theme of *For a Few Dollars More* and
Wagner's 'Ride of the Valkyries'! The
presence of dynamite in their saddles
(unknown to Jack) makes this easy, and
Jack visualises the incident making the
history books in a stunning use of slow-
motion photography and still-sepia repro-

duction of old dime novel covers. Like
No-Name in *For a Few Dollars More* Nobody
'supervises' the gundown, but his presence
in a train is more designed to make Jack
face the Wild Bunch rather than see fair
play is observed. All that is left is a staged
gundown between Jack and Nobody, in
which the former collapses, identically to
Frank in *Once Upon a Time in the West*.

The climax sees Jack about to sail to
Europe, writing a farewell letter to Nobody
leaving him the heritage of the 1899 West.
One interesting element at this point, is the
presence of a young Chinese boy at the
wharf gently teased by Nobody (Leone's
hint of the Italian Western Kung-Fu films
about to succeed Nobody). If *Once Upon a
Time in the West* was Leone's personal vision
and farewell to the world of the Italian
Western then *My Name is Nobody* is its
satirical counterpart. Unlike most comedy-
Italian Westerns the film is marvellously

5169-33

funny utilising the diverse talents of Terence Hill and the iconographical persona of Henry Fonda to the best possible advantage. With filmic references to elements of the American and Italian Western tradition, the Roman satirical tradition of the

Fonda as Jack Beauregarde in *My Name is Nobody*.

commercial film reaches its heights here. Though flawed in parts due no doubt to Valerii's direction, *My Name is Nobody* is an enjoyable provisional film until the completion of *Once Upon a Time – America*.

The Political Western

'Tell him the Swede is here'
            (Yod Peterssen in *Compañeros*)

In Italy, quite a number of the Westerns made had a political flavour, and were made under the guise of appeal to a mass audience. Though in many cases the political Western was just another gimmick employed by directors to add a new novelty to their films and had no real connection with the period of the West they were representing, still in a few cases an attempt was made to extend the directions of the Western in a more individual and political level. Directors such as Sergio Sollima, Damiano Damiani, and to a lesser extent, Sergio Corbucci, used the theme of the outcast, who was usually an illiterate Mexican peasant, and placed him in opposition to the developing racialistic force of capitalism then present in the Old West. Generally an outsider such as Sergei Kowalski in *A Professional Gun,* Yod

From *A Professional Gun.*

Peterssen in *Compañeros* or Ninio in *A Bullet for the General* would find his Eufemio, Vasco or Chuncho to take under his arm and educate into the intricacies of pragmatic revolutionary strategies away from naïve idealism for his own purposes. If this theme sounds familiar it should be remembered that both Franco Solinas and Giorgio Alorio who wrote the story for *A Professional Gun* also wrote *Quiemada!*. Solinas himself has contributed to the stories of Italian Westerns such as *The Big Gundown,* and was dialogue adapter on *A Bullet for the General*; it is interesting to find the same motifs cropping up in all three films such as the tuition of the inexperienced native by the experienced gringo and the final departure (in some cases prevented) of the gringo abroad at the climax of each film. When properly used, motifs of the political Western, can get the message through to a mass audience much better than any *Vent d'Est* of a Jean-Luc Godard.

From *A Bullet for the General*.

In an interview in June 1971 Sollima himself stressed that he made his Westerns as political allegories. Cucillo, the key figure of two of his Westerns, was symbolic of the exploitation of the underdeveloped Third World by the capitalist West. This is symbolised in the final gundown when Cucillo has only his knife to defend himself against his well-dressed, heavily armed gringo opponent. Yet as Cucillo usually wins in the end, despite the offer of a gun to even up the score (offered by Corbett in *The Big Gundown*), so eventually will the Third World rise up against Western imperialism. It is interesting to note here that Sollima shows the development of capitalism as represented by certain figures in his Westerns – the rancher (Walter Barnes) and the German mercenary in *The Big*

Gundown and Williams (Gianni Rizzo) who hires Beau for his dirty work in *Face to Face*.

With script by Sergio Donati and Sollima from a story by Solinas and Fernando Morandi, *The Big Gundown* is the first of Sollima's Westerns which oppose the institutional forces of law and order to the claims of simple justice. An honest, if unquestioning, lawman (Lee Van Cleef) is hired by rancher Walter Barnes to hunt down a degenerate Mexican (Tomas Milian) who has allegedly raped and murdered a young girl on the ranch. Corbett agrees and during the chase, in the course of the film, Sollima makes both Corbett and the audience gradually question the validity of Cucillo's guilt as with each step in the narrative a new factor is revealed which gradually undermines the conclusiveness of

Brad and Bean in *Face to Face*.

Brad and Pinkerton man in *Face to Face*.

Bean in *Face to Face*.

our previous judgement. Finally, when
Cucillo is cornered by a posse at the close of
the film, Corbett has become doubtful of
the whole set-up. Like another Sollima
figure such as Siringo in *Face to Face* he is
the third party in a conflict who has to
decide between the forces of law and order
which he serves and the justice which even a
Cucillo is entitled to. When the guilty
degenerate son-in-law of Barnes appears to
shoot Cucillo down, Corbett makes the
choice giving Cucillo a fighting chance.

As in *Face to Face* both men part at the
climax with a new respect for each other.

Stylistically and thematically, *Face to Face*
is one of the most important of the Italian
Westerns. Co-scripted again by Sollima
and Donati it is one of the most political of
his Westerns. Very reminiscent of *Performance*
the film questioned whether the subservience
to Western educational principles of
morality in a 'civilised' environment would
necessarily remain with a man in a different
situation. Paradoxically in *Face to Face* it is

the outcast Beau (Tomas Milian) who is the more moral figure at the climax of the film than the civilised Brad (Gian-Maria Volonté). The film opens with Brad Fletcher, a New England Professor, saying farewell to his class of students in a gloomy classroom with rain from a darkened sky beating at the windows. He has a terminal illness and must travel West for his health. Brad emphasises in this scene, which is essential for the rest of the film, that it is important to know oneself and to always do what is right. Later events are to prove that Brad is just an armchair moralist since the West is to put his dearly held principles to the test. That he believes himself a representative of justice and morality, is clear. The issue is whether he is capable of holding these principles in a different situation. Falling in with outlaw Beauregard Bennet, through force of circumstances, he finds himself gradually changing into a mirror image of Beau, though in a more corrupt manner. Beau begins as a savage outlaw figure who eventually reforms indirectly under Brad's influence, integrating the principles which Brad had purported to represent into himself. Thus the civilised distinction between law-abiding and lawlessness is rendered ambiguous at the climax of the film, since it is the outlaw who will prove the more moral of the two.

Brad slowly begins to assume leadership of Beau's gang and is responsible for a disastrous raid in which the latter is captured. The circumstances of his capture are interesting. In a town a young Mexican boy asks Beau (who is disguised as a Mexican), to play with him since the other American boys of the town do not. Here we have a parallel with Cucillo who is nearly always victimised by civilisation because he is Mexican. Beau is captured because he remains behind to help the boy, who is killed in the bank raid. Thus some form of morality is dawning in his mind since Brad's influence has begun to lead Beau to reflect on the circumstances of life which surround him.

The third figure in the film is represented by Pinkerton man Siringo (William Berger).

Like Corbett he is the representative of law and order concerned only to capture Beau, infiltrating his gang by very unorthodox methods. At the climax of the film he is left alone with Brad and Beau, having saved them from a vigilante posse in the desert. Despite his advice, the townspeople had organised a vigilante host which had massacred many innocent people at Beau's hideout. Brad is killed by Beau when he attempts to kill Siringo. Thus, like Corbett in *The Big Gundown,* Siringo is left with the decision between the claims of law and justice. He decides in favour of the latter, letting Beau go free since he has seen that the old Beauregard Bennet is now dead.

Sollima's third film *Run Man Run* with Tomas Milian again as Cucillo, was not released here, but the same thematic concerns as the above films were in evidence in a tale of a search for treasure to be used for the revolution. Like many directors, after finishing his Westerns Sollima moved on to crime films. *Revolver* (1973) with Fabio Testi and Oliver Reed, was a modern version of *The Big Gundown* involving the tale of a pursuit of an escaped anarchist throughout Europe by a prison warden. Some of the themes of Sollima's Westerns were seen in a developed form in *Violent City* (1970). The modern city could be seen as an evolution of the developing capitalism of the Old West now institutionalised as Big Business, as represented by Telly Savalas and Umberto Orsini viewed with disenchantment through the eyes of manipulated assassin Charles Bronson.

Sergio Corbucci is one of the most prolific directors in the Italian cinema and has worked in comedy, crime and historical films. In many films he exhibits a paradoxical mixture of vulgarity and thematic insight but any interesting development he might have made is often hampered by the fact that as an entertainment director he often will not scruple to inject any gratuitous element into his films. Nevertheless he has made some interesting ones.

Minnesota Clay (1964) was made at the same time as Leone's first Western but it was not until *Django* (1965) that his flair for

Cameron Mitchell in *Minnesota Clay.*

'Rescued' by the US Cavalry from *The Hellbenders*.

Westerns appeared. Franco Nero was seen in the classic iconographical mould of the hero with stubble, broad brimmed hat, black coat, wiping out Mexicans and Ku-Klux-Klan (the last with machine-gun concealed in a coffin). The interesting surrealistic colour photography was by Enzo Barboni, later E. B. Clucher of the Trinity films. After *Ringo and his Golden Pistol* (1966) he returned to the theme of the South in *The Hellbenders* (1966).

It is *The Hellbenders* that is one of Corbucci's most professionally accomplished films in both a coherent and thematic sense. There was none of the black humour

or oppressive surrealistic imagery which tended to mar his other work. Obviously designed as a Joseph Cotten vehicle to follow *The Tramplers* (1966), since the producer Alfred Band had also directed the earlier film with Joseph Cotten in a similar role as the fanatical Southern patriarch, *The Hellbenders* continued Corbucci's attack on the South in the framework of a perverse American dream. Set in the immediate aftermath of the Civil War, The Hellbenders is the name of a defunct Southern regiment now applied by Jonas (Joseph Cotten) its one-time leader to himself and his band of sons. He is a fanatic attempting to revive

The Coffin in *The Hellbenders*.

credits sequence it is shown to contain not a body but rifles and a whisky bottle. The latter belongs to Kitty, a drunken whore hired to impersonate the dead son's widow. Corbucci no doubt intends her to be a parody on the Southern gentlewoman. With the exception of Ben (Julian Mateos) the sons are murderous thugs with no real feeling for their father's cause, but are only interested in the money. Symbolic use is thus made of the coffin in the film in a death-re-birth theme. For Jonas, the money is to be used for the revival of the Southern cause, while for the other two sons the cause is already dead.

This symbolism is reinforced by certain sub-themes. When Kitty is murdered by one of Jonas' sons, Clare (Norma Bengell), a gambler from the same background as Kitty, is reluctantly recruited. This family unit of fanatical father, mock Southern gentlewoman, faithful son and treacherous brothers completes an ironic picture in terms of the iconography of the normal Western family. It is Ben's failure to break out of this vicious circle which causes both his and Clare's doom at the film's climax. Religion is also satirised for at the opening of the film, Jonas is seen leading his sons and hired helpers in prayer before the massacre. The latter are later murdered 'for the Cause'. As in *Django* the whole Southern ethos is shown to be corrupt. The Southern concept of honour is broken on two occasions in the film. When bandit Pedro (Aldo Sambrell) approaches with a white flag, he is cynically shot by Jonas, but when he and his band reach the coffin, they do not open it out of simple superstitious reverence, which is at least preferable to that of the Southerners' attitude. Again when the beggar (Al Mulock) arrives in Jonas' camp he is treated with contempt, in contradiction to the Southern code of hospitality.

The Hellbenders' thematic concerns are very reminiscent of the dimensions of Greek tragedy. All are doomed either through breaches of a code or inability to see the true motives of the other. Jonas is blind to

the lost Southern cause with money stolen from a Union detachment after a brutal massacre. In the course of the film a very intricate plot structure is revealed. The band are frequently challenged by posses, on the look-out for the killers of the Union detachment, and are nearly slaughtered by a gang of Mexicans from whom they are ironically rescued by the US Cavalry, and are torn with internal divisions. Corbucci's use of symbolism is succinctly apparent in the whole film. The lost cause motif appears early in the film since the money is transported in a coffin purporting to contain the body of one of Jonas' sons. At the prethe venality of his two sons, Clare believes Jonas to be a mere killer until she sees too late that he has his positive characteristics in living for a cause. Ben is a victim of the false idea of unity of the family. He attempts to keep it together even shielding the psychopathic brother from the justice of the Indians, but at the cost of his own life. The lizard on the flag draped over the coffin is also involved in the symbolic structure of the film. It may possibly be linked to the beggar's answer to the question as to where he came from: 'From under a rock. That's where they say we all began'. This may also be seen as an implicit criticism of *The Hellbenders* The lizard can be taken as symbolic of the family's hopes of reviving the Southern cause. As the flag is obviously the family crest, the lizard motif is correlated with Jonas' new order, a symbol of a reversal of evolution identified with Jonas at the film's climax.

With the help of the excellent photography of Enzo Barboni, the Hellbenders are normally seen isolated from society against a desert locale. Whenever they enter any boundary of civilised law and order, they are seen as anachronisms in the new post-Civil War America. In a predominantly Northern town they find a blind ex-Confederate, who knew the real deceased they purport to be carrying. He is accepted as one of the citizens in the town without any hint of prejudice. After being rescued

Clare and the blind Confederate in *The Hellbenders*.

by the US Cavalry the coffin is given an honourable burial in the fort at Clare's request. The role of Pedro also deserves some comment. Though appearing as a mere bandit Corbucci virtually depicts him in the guise of a Greek chorus, since just before he dies he utters a curse on Jonas, the 'man of honour' who shot him while carrying a white flag, thus sealing the doom of the enterprise. It is his body which is found in the coffin, which Ben and his brothers had taken from the cemetery by mistake. Thus seen in the context of the film his curse adds an almost supernatural dimension.

The final scene asserts the film's pessimism. Ben, mortally wounded as he is caught in the crossfire of his brothers'

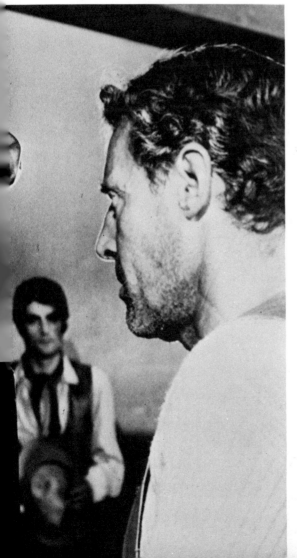

bullets, and Clare dying of pneumonia, can only watch as the now insane Jonas crawls across the mud flats like a lizard carrying the coffin's flag. As he reaches the river, the last barrier they had to cross, the dying Jonas casts in the flag which floats half-way across then sinks. This is a brilliant summation of the film's symbolism.

After *Navajo Joe* to the script of which Fernando di Leo contributed and which was also notable for the final gundown between Joe and Duncan (Aldo Sambrell) in an Indian graveyard, Corbucci made *The Grand Silence* (1968). Its chief merit lay in its inversion of the Western stereotype. Trintignant played a mute killer hired to stop the slaughter of an outlaw community in the snowy wastes by psychopathic bounty hunter Klaus Kinsky. As well as being notable for the appearance of Frank Wolff in the different role of an upright marshall the film's ending was one of the most unique in the whole Western field. With hands crushed and outnumbered by enemies, Trintignant is shot to death by Kinsky and his men. This ending was thought so shocking that when the film was re-released in France a more conventional ending was shot.

Corbucci's *A Professional Gun* (1968) was a key example of a commercial political Western. In early twentieth century Mexico, Sergei Kowalski (Franco Nero) sets out to exploit the political situation for his own advantage, but ends up coaching the idealistic Eufemio (Tony Musante) in the ways of revolutionary warfare just as does Sir William Walker (Marlon Brando) to José Dolores in *Quiemada!* Though we have a similarity in both films, it is difficult to know whether the Solinas-Alorio story has been preserved to their own satisfaction as the film is essentially a Corbucci entertainment Western directed in an exuberant manner and owing a lot to Leone's techniques. Frequent close-ups of the face and eyes occur with the obligatory gundown set in a circus ring. Eufemio in clown's outfit faces Curly (Jack Palance), an evil homosexual killer whom Corbucci has said is symbolic of the evils of capitalism, armed

with rifles, with Nero acting in a similar manner to Eastwood in *For a Few Dollars More*. Other features of the film are its comic strip direction, frequent zip-pans, excellent colour and camera movements of Alejandro Ulloa, and a blasphemous send-up of religion when Giovanni Ralli appears dressed as Christ in a religious festival, with Nero and Musante as angels so that they can conveniently machine-gun Government troops.

After *Drop Them or I'll Shoot* (1969) which Corbucci made merely as a Johnny Hallyday vehicle, he was back on form with *Compañeros* (1970) a much more professional version of the themes of *A Professional Gun*. This time Franco Nero appeared as cynical Swedish arms dealer Yod who has to accompany loutish bandit Vasco (Tomas Milian in a superb comedy performance) to rescue pacifist Professor Xantos (Fernando Rey) from US imperialists in Texas in order to gain supposed wealth. Opposing them is larger than life pot-smoking villain John the Wooden Hand (Jack Palance) who feeds his enemies to his pet falcon Marsha who had freed him from a cross by eating his hand! Since Nero had been responsible for this Palance's vendetta is indeed justified. *Compañeros* was an excellent comedy adventure which let its message of the futility of pacifism against US imperialism develop out of the context of the film.

Corbucci went on to make other films such as *What Have I to do with the Revolution?* with Vittorio Gassman, *The J and S Gang* with Tomas Milian and Susan George in the Western field. His eccentricity can threaten to get the best of him in film making, and he is at his best when in alliance with other talents on one of his projects, rather than being in full control.

Carlo Lizzani's *Requiescant* (1966) was one of the few Italian Westerns to take a positive view of religion, mainly because its central character, Lou Castel, is a priest, who with the aid of Don Juan (Pier Paolo Pasolini) assists the Mexican revolution against

Yod and John in *Compañeros*.

Tomas Milian as Vasco in *Compañeros*.

Castel and Volonté in *A Bullet for the General*.

wicked capitalists Mark Damon and Ninetto Davoli. Most Westerns use the theme of exploitation of the Mexicans indiscriminately as in *No Room to Die* and the political element is just there as a stock theme. Westerns have been made which satirised politics, as in Tessari's *Long Live Death . . . Preferably Yours!* (1971) with an all star cast of Franco Nero, Eli Wallach and Lyn Redgrave. If we close this section with a refer-ence to one of the best of the political Westerns then *A Bullet for the General* is the obvious choice.

Made in 1966 it was Damiano Damiani's only venture into the twentieth century Mexican Western field. In reality it is less a Western and more an allegory on South American politics related to Damiani's political interests which have been present from his neo-realist days. The plot involves

From *A Bullet for the General.*

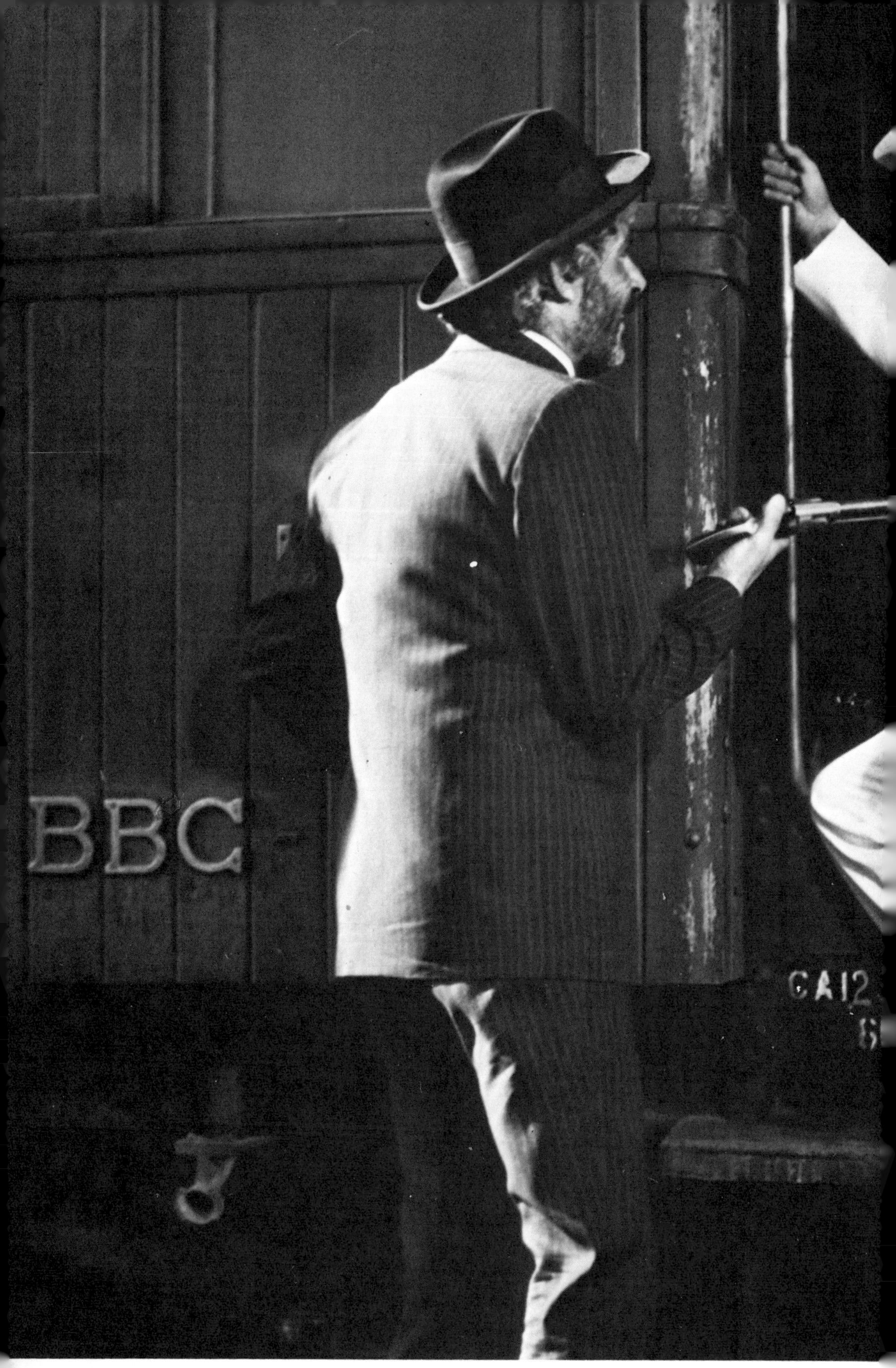
BBC
CA12

The final reckoning from *A Bullet for the General*.

the efforts of a mysterious, unemotional American (effectively played by Lou Castel) to infiltrate the gang of naïve, emotional El Chuncho (Gian-Maria Volonté) and gain access to the hideout of a revolutionary general. During the course of the film a Svengali process results, in which the child-like inexperienced Chuncho is gradually dominated by the experienced gringo so that he departs from his former honourable revolutionary ardour into the path of cold pragmatic strategy, ·which results in the loss of his gang and the hatred of his simple-minded brother (Klaus Kinsky). However, though he has been taken in, Chuncho manages to escape this 'imperialist' domination and return to his old life just in time.

With an exuberant performance by Volonté which is countered by the unemotional restrained playing of Castel *A Bullet for the General* succeeds, despite its truncated versions both here and in the States, in making its message clear. However, we are never certain if Castel is just a paid assassin or a US employee, and his motives remain obscure until half-way through the film when Volonté discovers the bullet meant for the General while Castel is suffering from malaria. Despite Castel's previous policy of non-involvement he forms an attachment with Volonté which is never satisfactorily explained in this edited version. But it his undoing. After explaining to Chuncho how he had taken him in he is surprised to see a gun pointing at him. Chuncho cannot explain why he has to kill him. He has shaken off his imperialist demon and kills him sending him back to America on the train. The last shot of him is a long shot. He has given his blood money to a poor man and divests himself of his Western clothes, calling for dynamite. There can be no doubt that this is the best use made of the political element in a Western and it is to be hoped that a complete version of *A Bullet for the General* will be made available one day.

Aftermath

The Italian Western had a relatively short life, as soon after 1970 many directors moved on to other concerns. For talents such as Damiani and Lizzani the Western had been just another genre to experiment with, while directors such as Corbucci and Sollima soon switched to other concerns in the Italian commercial cinema. Many other scriptwriters and directors had obviously worked in the Western to get commercial freedom, to make their own kind of films or merely to continue working in the film industry. Relevant examples are: Florestano Vancini who directed *The Long Days of Revenge* (1966) and who was later to move on to films such as *Violence Equals Power* and *The Matteoti Affair* (1974); Massimo Dallamano, who was Leone's director of photography on *A Fistful of Dollars* and *For a Few Dollars More* while also directing Westerns such as *Bandidos* (1968) and who was later to direct *Cosa Avete Fato a Solange?* (1972); and Tonino Cervi who directed the enigmatic *Queens of Evil* (1970) with Haydee Politeff. One of the most interesting and prolific scriptwriters in the field, Fernando di Leo, (who worked on *The Long Days of Revenge, Navajo Joe* (1966), *Seven Guns for the McGregors* (1965), *Seven Brides for the McGregors* (1966), *Sugar Colt* (1966), *Wanted* (1966) among many others) was later to move on to the field of crime and sexploitation films. Thus for the vast majority of directors and scriptwriters the Italian Western was just a way of earning a living until the next assignment; but a contribution was made by talents such as Tessari and Dario Argento (later to direct a trilogy of original crime thrillers *The Gallery Murders, Cat O' 9 Tails* and *Four Flies on Grey Velvet*) which was worth the excesses of the majority of bad Westerns – just as the discovery of a Cottafavi in the epic films was worth the presence of absurdities like *Hercules Against the Moon Men!*

However the American cinema was quick enough to jump on the bandwagon with cheap imitations of the Italian Western. Among the most excruciating examples were films like *Hang 'Em High,* directed by the second-rate Ted Post, *More Dead than Alive, Five Savage Men* and *A Town Called Bastard. Hang 'Em High* was Eastwood's first film on his return to America. As well as reverting to the old Western stylised costumes, it attempted to cash in on the violence of the Italian Western. Finally the end product was more grotesque, cheap and nasty, and more symptomatic of the sickness of the American cinema than of the ability of the Italian Western to use violence in a subtle and justifiable way, under better directors. Even a John Wayne film was not exempt. His *Big Jake* (1970) had not only Richard Boone in a poncho but a villian similar to Bud Spencer, and an increased use of violence in the opening scene. This was more derivative in the American cinema than in the Hong Kong Kung-Fu films which borrowed some of the visuals and even the Morricone scores of Italian Westerns. Fortunately this trend has died down.

If there is one thing of value which the Italian Western will have contributed, it is the recognition of the power of visuals and soundtrack as well as narrative in the media of the Western. Without the sometimes erratic presence of the whole genre, the American Western would have been doomed to further sterility and unrealistic stylisation which would have deterred any originality developing in that media. Peckinpah's *The Wild Bunch* undoubtedly bears signs of the influence of the Italian Western, but used in an original way: Not only is it set in the period of Corbucci's *A Professional Gun* with even a reference to an aeroplane (which appears in the former film), but it has an imaginative use of a gundown motif with Ernest Borgnine, Warren Oates, Ben Johnson and William Holden walking in silence down a Mexican street with a sound-

track beating a Mexican death requiem. **Richard Boone in *Big Jake*.**
Since Leone satires Peckinpah in *My Name is Nobody* such borrowings may well have been intentional.

Though short-term, the Italian Western's influence has been beneficial in spite of the excesses. With a greater use of realism and violence in the Western cinema and a discarding of stylistic sterility, the way has been paved not only for future international cinema developments in the genre, but also the liberation of any innovations from the oppression of cliché. Innovations were attempted in the past with little success so perhaps the way is now open for a greater tolerance and experimentation in the whole Western field.

PART II
THE OPERA OF VIOLENCE

Western into Opera

When reading a book on the films of Alfred Hitchcock one would be surprised to see a large section devoted to the film music of Bernard Hermann. When reading a book on the American Gangster film or the American Western one would not expect to find a special section on the music of Tiomkin, Devol, Bernstein or any other. Why then does a book on the Italian Western have a section which deals specifically with the contribution made by the film composer? For that matter, why not a section dealing with the camera crew, make-up, photography or even locations?

A parody of 'The Ride of the Valkyries' may be heard in *My Name is Nobody*.

It is in this chapter that we hope to point out, that the role of the film composer in the Italian Western is quite unique. Never before, in the history of film, has the composer been brought forward to such a significant position for an entire genre of film.

One cannot pretend to have an explanation as to why the composer should have occupied such a significant position in the production of the Western, but by taking a retrospective look at the Italian Western, bearing in mind the legacy of Italian music,

the role seems to be one of natural evolution.

The Italian Western simply provided a vehicle for cinematic opera. Opera: 'Dramatic performance of composition of which music is an essential part.' (Oxford Dictionary). Several hundreds of Westerns have been made in Italy and they do not all have affiliations with Verdi, but for a large majority of the *significant* productions music is an essential part.

The evolution should not necessarily be a surprising one. After all, Italy is the home

of the opera and the bonds and seeds of heritage cannot be ignored. Many Italian film composers (for example Bruno Nicolai and Ennio Morricone) have written for the theatre, to say nothing of the various directors whose roots are in the stage. In listening to Morricone's score for *My Name is Nobody*, the strains of *The Ride of the Valkyries* can be heard. Although intended as an ironic touch is it not also perhaps a significant one?

This affiliation may be seen in many other Italian films such as the partnership of Fellini and Nino Rota, but it was not until the Western came along, that the affiliation reached a prominent position. The reason is simple. The specifically *Italian* treatment of the subject: Western (until then an essential *American* subject), became transformed by the natural Italian dramatic heritage into the essence of opera. In short, the Western Italian style provided a perfect vehicle for *operatic moments*.

What exactly is meant by this, will be discussed later, but at the moment let it suffice to say that in the Italian Western we have a positively unique example of a high level of musical integration with that of the action.

In the Italian Western there is a whole spectrum of activity that has curious links with that of opera. There is both comedy and tragedy – tragedy which at some points approaches that of the Classical. There is struggle for survival – one has only to examine the levels of emotional encounter in *Once Upon a Time in the West* to appreciate exactly what one is dealing with. It is no surprise that in an edition of the London magazine *Time Out* Leone's masterpiece was referred to as Leone's opera.

Particularly significant in my Western-Opera equation are the various stock moments in the Italian Western which lend themselves to significant 'moments'. These can be listed: revelations, encounters, ordeals involving physical brutality and finally, the apex of the Italian Western-Opera *La Resa Dei Conti* – the gundowns – the settling of accounts. Certainly there are gunfights in American Westerns, but never

on the scale and 'grandness' of the Italian Western.

The whole field of Italian Western production is like that of a tightly knit repertory company. Familiar faces crop up all the time, similar banks are robbed in different films. Whole camera crews may work for several directors, almost at the same time. The Italian Western has evolved stock characters such as Terence Hill, Giuliano Gemma, and Mario Brega. Likewise a stock of film composers evolved, almost all of whom lived and worked in and around Rome. Many of these composers shared studios, worked in each other's orchestras, belonged to the same company and so on. So great is the degree of musical integration in Italy that we may begin to talk of a 'school of Italian film music'.

It is not therefore surprising to find that Bruno Nicolai may conduct for Carlo Rustichelli, play organ for Ennio Morricone whilst writing his own score for *A Man Called Apocalypse Joe!* Nicolai is merely a case in point. A choir heard on a Morricone score, a Rustichelli score and a Fidenco score will almost certainly be Allessandroni's Cantori Moderni. The use of a female voice on a score will amost certainly be that of Edda Dell'Orso, the sound of a whistling man will certainly be Allessandroni. All of these superb musicians and composers are like one large family (very like the opera tradition).

Because of the repertory nature of the Italian Western, it is not surprising to find that there are times when there is a marked similarity not only in certain tableaux in the films themselves, but also in the actual scoring of the film. In fact, just as in opera, certain musical conventions evolved from the genre to which many composers conformed. These similarities have resulted in criticisms, but once the conditions are appreciated then the situation is more easily understood. In one case many people in Great Britain and the USA were convinced that Morricone and Nicolai were one and the same person because of similarities in their music.

Many Italian Western scores sound very

Terence Hill

Giuliano Gemma.

similar. Cracking whips, bells, chants, fuzzy guitar passages and solo whistling is not merely an Ennio Morricone trademark, it is the trademark of a peculiarly original kind of scoring, and a type that is unique to the Italian Western. Alan Warner of United Artists once said about the score *Indio Black*: 'It's by Bruno Nicolai, though it could be Morricone . . . at any rate you can be damn sure it's not Percy Faith.'

There is the case of an Italian composer (who shall remain nameless) who was asked over the telephone to write a score for 'a love story' with a 'hit main theme' plus a 'considerable amount of *lush* strings'. This particular composer never saw the film, read a script or even met the producer. The final product actually worked, with very little adjustment necessary and the American film for which it was written was indeed a success. This is one approach to film scoring and one which many American composers use, although of course they usually read the script. Scores may also be written with the composer actually watching shots – indeed many are conducted with a screen above the orchestra. However, with the Italian Western occasionally quite a different technique is adopted. To quite a considerable extent, *Once Upon a Time in the West* was made around Morricone's music and ideas. The watch melody in *For a Few Dollars More* gave Leone the idea of using a sound effect both in the concrete sense and the metaphysical sense. Consequently it was from this idea that the harmonica theme evolved in *Once Upon a Time in the West*. Much of the film was constructed on this idea. As a result we can see a very deep involvement of the composer with the film, to the extent that Francesco De Masi and Carlo Rustichelli painstakingly record every accompanying one or two bars for merely a few frames of film. In the Italian Western the music is not merely background but a highly integrated prominent element. Just as there would be no opera if there was no music, there would be no true Italian Western without the score.

'You can be damn sure it's not Percy Faith'

To appreciate the concise individuality of Italian Western scoring it will be a useful exercise to take a look at some examples of scoring for the American Western, and its gross imitator the German Western.

Dimitri Tiomkin's score for *The Alamo*, whilst being a magnificent piece of writing reflected a typical American Western;

sentimentality in 'The Green Leaves of Summer', a cowboy choir crooning in the background. Listen to the lyrics of some of the songs: 'Tennessee babe with the sweet sounding name . . .' and particularly from 'The Ballad of the Alamo' – '. . . a small band of soldiers are asleep in the arms of the Lord . . . you can hear them in the roll call in the sky . . . thirteen days of Glory at the siege of Alamo'. In Leone's *The Good, the Bad, and the Ugly* there is no glory. The senselessness of the Civil War is pointed out in many instances and Morricone's 'The Story of a Soldier', whilst a very sweet melody almost in *Alamo* tradition, certainly does not sing of the 'Thirteen Days of Glory'.

Let us look at some of the tradition of the American Western, the music of which has its grass roots in a lot of folk song. As the credits for *The Range Rider* loom upon the screen and we are introduced to 'Dick West all-American boy' we are treated to a chorus of 'Home, home on the range, where the deer and the antelope play' . . . Remember the range in *Once Upon a Time*, but then Leone was talking about just that . . . ONCE UPON A TIME. The Lone Ranger galloped across the screen in time to the 'William Tell Overture' – or at least a corrupted version, with an interjected 'Hi Ho Silver!' Here we are in the world of the comic strip Western – a fact realised by many Italian composers. Musical scores like Victor Young's *Shane* although extremely beautiful have the unmistakable American stamp of being *American heroic*. This quality can be seen in much of Tiomkin's work also. Any change that may be discerned in American scoring may be noticed after Leone. When Germany started to make Westerns after the American style, the German composer Martin Böttcher wrote in a very American style. Böttcher's music, whilst being extremely good, is unmistakably that of the Heroic West – grandeur, an occasional background of tom-toms – Monument Valley is almost visible merely from listening to a dozen or so bars.

It is even possible to see this kind of scoring in some of the early Italian Westerns

The range in *Once Upon a Time in the West*.

German composer Bottcher wrote in a very American style – note comment on poster.

and in one or two of the later ones after Italy had so obviously cultivated its own style.

Early Italian Westerns such as *Massacro Al Grande Canyon* (music Gianni Ferrio), *Buffalo Bill L'Eroe del Far West* (music by Carlo Rustichelli), *Tre Dollari di Piombo* and *Le Maledette Pistole de Dallas* (composed by Angelo), as well as having strikingly American titles all have scores which although possessing their own particular individuality, bear much of the 'American stamp' rather than the later 'Italian'. Early Italy produced *Massacre at the Grand Canyon,* and later Italy *I'll Call on Your Widow on my Way Home!*

What happened, then, in Italy to produce a unique approach to film scoring of Westerns? Important directors such as

Leone have already been mentioned, now let us mention the name of one particular film composer: Ennio Morricone. Morricone, without deriding the tremendous talent of a large number of other Italian film composers, is probably the most important name in the field of Italian film music. Morricone's contribution to the Italian cinema, not only in the field of the Western is immense, to say the least. His praises as a film composer have been sung far and wide by such notable personalities as Leone, Sollima, Corbucci, Montaldo and Petrie . . . to name a few.

In the same way that Leone gave the American Western a shot in the arm, then Morricone gave film scoring a booster which was to prove particularly significant to the Western. Were you to ask a member of the general public who knew a little about film scoring, who Morricone was, the majority would reply 'He is an Italian who writes music for Westerns', and indeed it is in the Western field that his greatest contribution is recognised. Unfortunately many people do not know enough about the man himself and the great contribution that he has made to many types of music. Few realise that it is primarily through his experimental work, that he has been able to achieve what he has, in the field of writing for the cinema.

The significant point to make is that it was primarily Morricone's contribution that brought about the change in style of film scoring for the Italian Western – in effect Morricone started a trend in Italian scoring.

It is sometimes difficult to identify a piece of music as being by Morricone or Nicolai, or such artistes as Nico Fidenco. It is equally difficult to state whether a particular composition has been directly influenced by Morricone or by the 'school' of Italian composers. Unfortunately we find ourselves in something of a circle since *both* Morricone and Bruno Nicolai worked under Maestro Godfredo Pertrassi whilst students... 'who influences whom?'

The music of Italian Westerns is unique and original. The majority of Italian Western scores are distinctly remote from the traditional cowboy influence of the fifties American scoring. A harmonica, whilst being a traditional cowboy instrument, takes on a greater and rather sinister significance in the hands of Ennio Morricone or Luis Enriquez. The strains of a spanish guitar 'have something to do with death' in the world of the Italian Western, a jaw harp becomes aural black comedy and the soul of Allessandroni's Cantori Moderni grabs the whole Western genre by the throat.

Ordinary musical instruments become representational and thus adopt a new form. Whistling, for example, is an established feature of what might be called cowboy music, happy carefree and a symbol of the

Morricone's contribution to the Italian cinema is immense, to say the least. Author, Laurence Staig, with Ennio Morricone in Rome.

126

Anthony, in *Blindman*, makes cynical comment to the accompaniment of a typical 'surrealist shriek' on the sound-track.

all American cow-boy. In the hands of Bruno Nicolai or Ennio Morricone a complete metamorphosis takes place. What we may traditionally associate with 'When Johnny Comes Marching Home' becomes a sinister death knell in *Il Mercenario*. Franco Nero played the ominous mercenary, whose whistling signature became an overture of death. The Bolero of a Spanish guitar announces a duel of death, as do the call of trumpets. Fuzzy guitars and jangling harpsichords take on individual musical identities. In a word, music becomes *symbol*, it adopts a signature in the same way that a poncho and a cigar do. As soon as two men meet and significant accompanying bars are heard, then the symbols have joined for *La Resa dei Conti*.

Many Italian composers are highly experimental. As well as instruments being put to unusual uses, the instruments themselves become integrated with the action. There are examples of this on many different levels. Signature pieces are used, unusual sounds capture specific feel – for example the piercing cry in *The Good, the Bad and the Ugly* and the gasping effect used in *A Man, a Horse and a Gun*. Music becomes a very real part of the story – the Harmonica in *Once Upon a Time in the West* and the watch melody in *For a Few Dollars More*.

It culminates in a musically surrealistic panorama of strange cries, savage guitar chords, jangling bells and the cracking of whips. Grunts, groans and Indian-like shrieks adorn the panorama. The form is totally unlike anything American. The music is as hostile as the action, the close affiliation enters the realm of Opera.

Allessandro Allessandroni: whistler, guitarist, vocalist, composer and leader of the superb Cantori Moderni.

'When the chimes end... pick up your gun'

Aural integration of music, in the Italian Western, has already been briefly mentioned but this integration process goes even further, some Western scores also extend to a visual element.

In many early American Westerns it was not unusual for the main musical theme of the film to be played on an old piano in a saloon sequence – the point being that the theme was SEEN to be played. This feature was to be adopted in several early Italian Westerns and used in films such as *The Rope and the Colt*. However, in the Italian Western we may see an extension of this idea, so that musical instruments themselves and the themes they play take on a prominent significance.

It is difficult to say who originated this technique, but it seems likely that it was a combination of Ennio Morricone and Sergio Leone. This links up with the idea of using a sound in both the real and the metaphysical sense of which Morricone often talks. This technique also helps to place the role of the film score firmly in perspective. In many Italian Westerns the music is the film, and therefore the introduction of actual musical instruments into the film should not be surprising.

In *For a Few Dollars More* Indio has a fetishist obsession, which involves his playing a musical watch before he draws on a victim. In the final sequence of the film when Indio faces the Colonel, the musical watch is produced with the words: 'When the chimes end . . . pick up your gun, try and shoot me Colonel.' This confrontation has a dual importance musically. Firstly it is the moment of truth, *La Resa dei Conti*, which is the natural conclusion to many Italian Westerns – a moment when the role

of the composer really asserts itself. Secondly, it is a moment when the true significance of the watch is realised – the watch not only acts as symbol but also spins the web of the film. The watch is *musical* – this is very important because it gives Morricone's score an even greater significance – a musical instrument plus its theme is the cornerstone of the entire film. The musical theme that is heard on the watch throughout the film, separates and becomes a grand finale in the final gundown.

A similar kind of process also occurred in the other Leone/Morricone collaboration *Once Upon a Time in the West*. Charles Bronson's harmonica theme worked in a very similar way to Gian-Maria Volonté's watch theme. Bronson even adopts the name of the instrument and he is known as Harmonica throughout the film. The whole film has a pervading atmosphere of unreality. Bronson wanders in and out of the action playing a strange bizarre tune which has no tune. His harmonica is his signature and his reason for being there, the reason for the film. Again, this is an example of an instrument and its theme dominating the action. In the final gundown sequence – *La Resa dei Conti* – Leone presents us with a vision, totally unreal but dramatically effective, and Morricone's almost surreal score crescendoes to a climax, based upon the role of the harmonica throughout the film. The harmonica is very important in *Once Upon a Time in the West*. It symbolises an old debt and is finally thrust into the dying Frank's mouth at the end of the film in reply to his 'Why . . .?'

In *The Good, the Bad and the Ugly* a slight variation on the old piano idea was seen in the instance of the song 'The Story of a

'Musical Fetish' – the watch from *For a Few Dollars More*.

In *Once Upon a Time in the West,* the harmonica symbolises an old debt which is finally thrust into Frank's mouth.

Franco de Gemini – the brilliant harmonica player in *Once Upon a Time in the West*.

The villains wait to draw, as the hotel orchestra plays, in *Revenge at El Paso*.

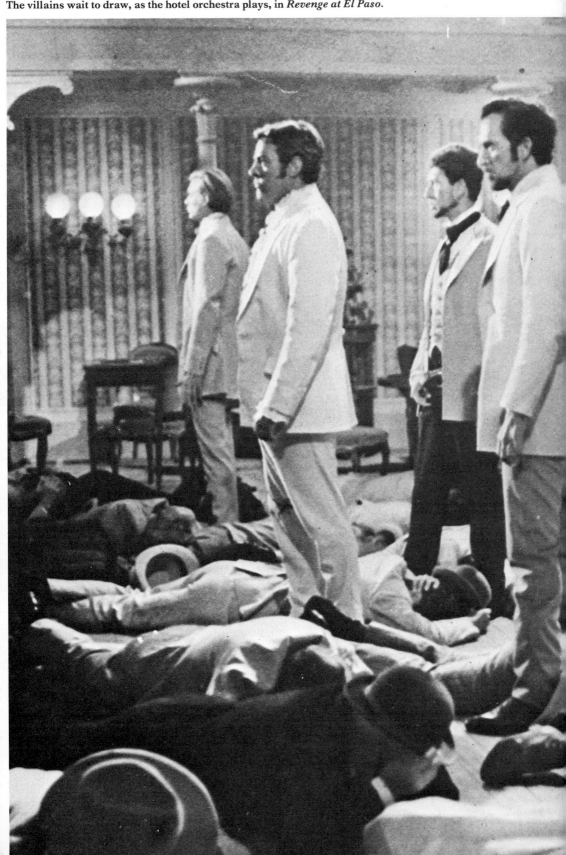

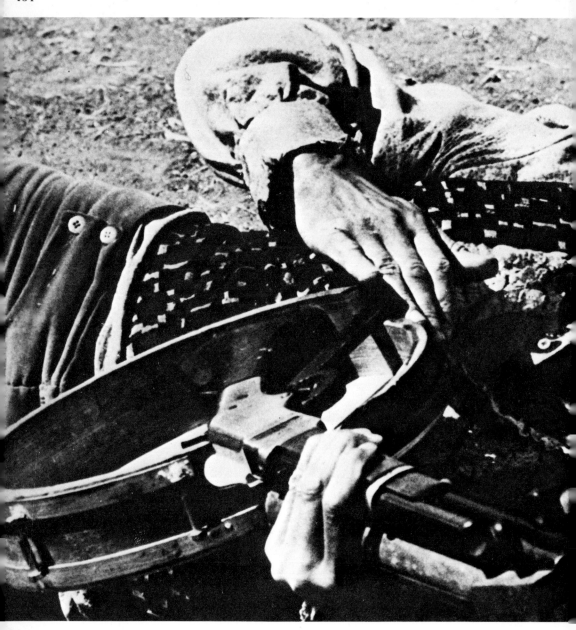

Soldier'; a very sweet melody which was sung by civil war prisoners outside the officer's hut, while Tuco was being practically beaten to death by Mario Brega. Leone cleverly interspersed the shots of Tuco's beating with the scenes of the soldiers' band playing outside. The musical effect was quite unique. The music was very sweet, almost straight out of an American film but the lyrics were highly anti-war and very unlike anything that might be found in *The Alamo*. As well as this, the accompaniment of ballad to beating, produces an ironical effect.

A soundtrack collector listening to the LP soundtrack of the film *La Collina Degli Stivali (Boot Hill)* would probably wonder if he had bought Nino Rota's *I Clowns*. This is not because of any similarity with Rota's music, but because most of the score by Carlo Rustichelli consists of circus music. Here again is another variation on the piano idea. As in *The Good, the Bad and the Ugly* with soldier musicians, there is rather an oblique accompaniment to action. The circus theme takes on rather sinister connotations and again the musicians may be seen

Banjo with his concealed shotgun in *Sabata*.

into the action — a slight variation on the usual convention of gundown music accompanying the draw. We have Indio's watch, Harmonica's harmonica, the circus band which crescendoes to the draw and the hotel band. Perhaps the height of this type of convention can be seen in a film by Frank Kramer — *Sabata*.

Sabata has at least three variations on the idea of using actual musical instruments and their themes in the action. The main anti-hero of the film is a character, played by William Berger, who goes under the name of Banjo — (shades of Harmonica?). Surprisingly enough . . . Banjo walks around playing a banjo. When gunfights take place Banjo often plays his opponents a little tune before firing. Here we again have a classic case of instrument involvement, but to a greater degree, because Banjo has a cleverly concealed sawn-off shotgun hidden . . . in his banjo!

Marcello Giombini wrote the excellent score to the film, and the theme which Banjo plays is often heard in many forms throughout the film. Banjo also wears jingling bells on his trouser legs, and consequently Giombini incorporates these sounds in his theme to give yet another example of this process of integration.

Banjo is quite a talented man. In a scene in the church, he is seen playing the organ. When a killer walks in, a small trap door opens at the base and a rifle opens out. Yet again we have constant music, culminating in the gunfight.

Not surprisingly, the time had to come when a parody would be made of these conventions, and significantly it is made by the man who was one of the innovators — Ennio Morricone. In his score to the Tonino Valerii film *My Name is Nobody* (itself a parody on the Trinity films) Morricone includes a gundown piece with . . . an alarm clock instead of a musical watch, a variation on the gundown theme in *How the West was Won* for Henry Fonda, and a Spanish guitar piece straight out of *The Good, the Bad and the Ugly*. We have come full circle.

playing the theme.

In the Carlo Rustichelli scored film *I Quattre dell'Ave Maria (Revenge at El Paso)* there is again a team of musicians playing the main theme but this time under familiar, conventional circumstances. In the last fifteen minutes of the film we witness a gundown between the *good* and the *bad*. Eli Wallach faces his enemies across a roulette table, a ball is spun in the wheel and Wallach requests that the hotel orchestra play a tune — when the ball settles they fire. Again, the introduction of actual musicians

The gundown in *My Name is Nobody*. **Morricone's score parodies his own conventions; we have come full circle**

'Tema di Johnny'

Something has already been shown of the Italian film composers' love of using unusual instruments and experimentation to produce new and novel sounds. Mention should now be made of the ways in which this technique is adopted into the sound-track.

In Italian Western film scoring, far more than in American film scoring we can see the technique of the adoption of certain set signature pieces and instrumental sounds to indicate certain characters and ideas. This is by no means a new technique. In Prokofiev's score for *Alexander Nevsky* there are separate themes for the Teutonic Knights and the villagers, as John Barry's James Bond scores have signatures for Bond. The point however is that in Italian Western scoring there seems at times to be a more prolific and more specialised technique. The identification of characters by certain pieces of music is as old as opera and it should not be assumed that I am making a case for crediting this technique to the western. An examination of this technique in operation however, uncovers an ingenious technique, which when adopted in a Leone film for instance, provides moments of high comedy and tragedy. A considerable amount of Leone's black humour may be credited to his film composer.

In *For a Few Dollars More*, the film opened to the sound of an ingenious Morricone score, which adopted the sound of a whistling man with an established Sicilian folk instrument, the jaw harp. The whistling theme was not new to Dollar fans since we had already come across this in the previous *A Fistful of Dollars*. What was unique however, was the idea of taking these two instruments from the signature piece, and using them separately during the film. Thus in scenes when Colonel Mortimer ominously appears on the scene, the sound-track produces an almost ominous twang of jaw harp – which combined with Van Cleef's smile produces quite a startling effect. Likewise we come to identify the whistle with the man with no name, as again the musical watch becomes identified with Indio and a variation of the melody is ominously linked with Mortimer for reasons that unfold within the story. This technique of the identification of strange sounds with certain characters, is a technique of Morricone's which can be seen at work in many other films. In certain scenes in the dollar films the technique of sound punctuation produces some remarkable moments which only go to demonstrate the remarkable team work of Leone and Morricone.

In *The Good, the Bad and the Ugly* the main theme is constantly punctuated by a strange high pitched vocal shriek which is the remarkable voice of Allessandro Allessandroni. In the opening fifteen minutes Tuco hurls himself through a window – the shot freezes as the words *Il Brutto* appear on the screen – but we are very aware of the strange, almost prophetic, shriek that we hear on the soundtrack. Likewise variations on this simple melody are heard, when we are introduced to the other two major characters in the story. The film must be viewed to see this amazing punctuation at work.

As I have taken pains to mention, the Italian cinema revels in imitation and the Stelvio Cipriani score to *Blindman* provides the closest link with the kind of scoring evident in *The Good, the Bad and the Ugly*. The score is good, very good, but the technique is basically Morricone's and Leone's. Anthony makes small witty comments which are followed with the shriek and familiar chanting characteristic of the score.

In the series of *Alleluja* Westerns for which Cipriani scored, there is also the signature innovation at work. The score which followed the first *Alleluja* film also included a variation on the previous main theme, which became George Hilton's theme.

Many Italian composers are very fond of adopting a whistling theme as a signature for a character. Morricone is particularly fond of this. In *Once Upon a Time in the West* there were many examples of this kind of film scoring. Jill had her own soaring female vocal piece which gave her 'Jill's theme'. Cheyenne had a slow-trot of a theme played on a banjo with a whistling accompaniment. On the LP soundtrack this is designated 'Addio Cheyenne'. Likewise Bronson had his sinister melody and Harmonica identification.

In *A Professional Gun* Morricone devised a very ingenious whistling melody which became the signature piece of Franco Nero as Il Mercanario. The theme also became prominent in gunfights and other such confrontations. Even before Nero had come into camera shot, his announcing melody prepared the viewer. Nero became transformed into Il Pinguino in Corbucci's film *Compañeros* and again a plodding whistling and banjo melody became his signature.

The whistling technique may also be seen in Bruno Nicolai's score for *Indio Black*, in which the theme designates Yul Brynner. *A Roof for a Skyful of Stars* and *What am I doing in the Revolution* all use this technique. Allessandroni is never short of commissions.

A perusal through a handful of Italian Western LP soundtrack albums will validate the point of the chapter. Over and over again the familiar words *Tema di . . . .* may be seen, to say nothing of the LPs where the word *Tema* is simply not designated. Johnny, in the film *Dirty Story of the West* has a special Francesco De Masi guitar riff which occurs twice, once in vocal format and secondly as the acknowledgement that this section of music is his identity.

Musical identity is very pronounced in *Sabata*. Banjo is identified by a ukelele melody, the villain Stengel by a trumpet dirge with a backing of 'thrilling' strings. . . . Sabata himself is identified by a very bouncy guitar twanging theme.

In *John the Bastard* we have a jerky theme

with a typical Allèssandroni choir backing which becomes 'Tema di John'. In *Rainbow* the LP credits a number of tracks to the various names of the characters, likewise a perusal of Western collection albums give us John, Charlie, Lo Straniero and Uncle Tom Cobbly and all as each having their individual musical signatures.

A quick look through the many scores written for American Westerns will soon reveal that although there is some degree of theme identification, which is an obvious feature of writing for action, the style does not approach the mastery of musical punctuation and signature writing that exists in the Italian cinema.

The sheer professional mastery of this technique is a contributing factor to the success of many Italian Westerns and in cases such as Leone and Corbucci is almost the substance of the film.

In Sollima's *La Resa dei Conti (The Big Gundown)* there are frequent shots of Cucillo fleeing from his pursuers to the shriek of a flute – Cucillo's theme, which identifies him as the pursued and hunted. The amalgamation of heavy percussion and trumpet during the chase sequences presents an aural landscape that tells the story just as much as the visual action. It has been said that listening to a well composed soundtrack, the action will convey itself through the music. This statement may be continually verified through the media of the Italian Western.

The villain Stengel in *Sabata*.

'Monty and Ted riding across the plains'

A genre as huge as the Italian Western with its American legacy – complete with 'star system' and 'spangled banner' must surely produce its peculiarities. Many Italian Westerns are purely bad cinema, and many Western soundtracks are very poor – but significantly this usually happens when they enter the realms of American imitation. There are occasions when the soundtrack almost becomes Range Rider-style Comic Strip, and sometimes the Italian Western's own unique style of composing reaches into self-parody. Thus the Italians themselves have produced their own unique style of 'comic strip'.

We must again remind ourselves of the musical legacy which came from the American Western. In the fifties it was not unusual for a vocal refrain to accompany the main theme of a Western. Thus we have:

– The man from Laramie, he had so many notches on his gun . . . Danger was this man's destiny, but you'd never cross the man from Laramie –
– Do not forsake me oh my darlin', on this our wedding day . . . sometime awhile whilst in State Prison said it's going to be my life or his and see that big hand movin' along, nearing High Noon –
– Keep movin' movin' movin', though they're disreputin', keep them dogies movin', Rawhide. Through rain and wind and weather, hell bent for leather wishin' my girl was by my side. –
– Boot Hill, Boot Hill, so quiet so still, where they lay side by side, the gunmen who died in the Gunfight at OK Corral. –
– I came to Town to search for gold, alookin' for a memory . . . so hang your dreams on the hangin' tree.–

All of the above quotes must be familiar. *Rawhide, High Noon, The Hangin' Tree* and so on, all from Westerns of the fifties which are also recognised as classics of their type. Vocalists Tex Ritter and Frankie Lane were introduced at celebrity meetings complete with gunslinging gear.

Then there is *Rin-Tin-Tin, Hopalong Cassidy* (clippitty clippitty clop!), *The Range Rider, The Cisco Kid, The Lone Ranger,* etcetera. The point must surely have been made. A substantial amount of the legacy of the American (and to some small extent British) Western was that of pure 'schoolboy fantasy'. How would these films have been viewed had they appeared after the Italian Western?

In the same way that star vocalists were produced from many American and British Westerns, an attempt was made to evolve a similar system with some of the Italian Westerns. It must always be borne in mind, that however unique the Italian Western is, at the back of every Italian mind must be the looming vision of Monument Valley.

Some of the earliest Italian Westerns, whilst having their own inimitable stamp, were still basic imitations of the American. Thus the scores to *Massacro Al Grande Canyon* and *Le Maledette Pistole di Dallas* still had relations with the traditional American form. It is difficult to account for the American bend in scoring, but I think it can be assumed that there are a few basic reasons for this. Firstly, there is the factor that the Italian Western was an innovation and This must have involved a lot of basic insecurity. This is exemplified by people like Leone, Morricone and Volonté changing their names to American pseudonyms. Even in the last two years many directors, actors, and composers still adopt aliases . . . Frank Kramer, Lee Beaver, Frank Mason, Anthony Dawson and Montgomery Wood, and so on. Even today the Italians are very conscious of American Western tradition.

Secondly, whatever one thinks of the

American Western, it was generally very successful and many seemed to adhere to basic formulas. Therefore it is not surprising ·that the Italians should choose to interpret one of these formulas.

Thirdly, as with the American Western, there was the opportunity to capitalise on the star system . . . and this they attempted to do.

Many Italian Westerns have vocal accompaniment to the main theme, which is usually heard while the credits loom upon the screen. A vast majority of these lyrics are in English, the reason being that there is a sincere attempt to emulate the American tradition. When a disc is available from a film, there may often be two versions of the song, one in Italian and one in English. When there is only one then usually the lyrics are in English even though the disc would not be distributed outside Italy (in some cases the *film's* distribution is confined to Italy).

The Italian attempt to emulate the American Western lyric is a pitifully sad one. Many of the lyrics are banal and a complete antithesis not only to the remarkable music that they accompany but also, and more significantly, to the actual film itself. However, this must be viewed in two

Record sleeves of some Italian Western sound-tracks *below and next page*

ways. Firstly, the lyrics are so bad (possibly unnoticed by an audience of non-English speaking Italians in a cinema in Milan), that they just totally disconnect from the film and are regarded as an unfortunate attempt at imitation. Secondly, curiously enough, the lyrics take on an aspect of black comedy. Here exists an almost traditional Western vocal refrain, accompanying a vision of the West which is quite opposite to that traditionally presented in the cinema. In effect there are times when the lyrics parody the very form which they had intended to copy.

But mention must be made of the lyrics which are quite unique. A message is put forward akin to Italian Western thinking such as in the song 'Run Man, Run', from *The Big Gundown,* or the violence of the lyric in *The Son of Django,* and the vocals in *Corri Uomo Corri.*

Many of the vocalists who sing the songs use American names. Mary Ure, Don Powell, Peter Tevis (who is American), Peter Boon (and the Dodge City Rangers!), and John Balfour. It must however also be mentioned, that a great number of the vocalists on Italian Western main titles are also well-known, prominent Italian 'pop' vocalists. To mention a few: Rita Pavone,

Roberto Matano, Maurizio Graf, Marco Bezzi, Peppino Gagliardi, Nico Fidenco (also a very important composer) and Fred Bongusto. At the height of its popularity in Italy many well-known Italian artists would produce a 'single from the current Italian Western' much in the same way that we had 'Rawhide' and 'The Man from Laramie' in the early fifties in England and the USA. The cover of the 45 would depict a reproduction of the publicity poster, plus an inset photograph of the recording artist. In several cases one would find a photograph of the actual recording artist in cowboy fringe, hat and holster! In Italy the Italian

Western was cult and as with every promotion a small star recording system came into existence. For Mario Bava's *Roy Colt and Winchester Jack* the main title was composed and sung by an Italian pop group.

Some Italian Western lyrics had meaning, genuine pathos. Most however were banal. Gianni Ferrio composed a very efficient (musically) score for *Vive e Preferibilimente Morte,* but the lyrics have to be heard to be believed. The lyrics take the form of a musical narration of the story. Album track titles include: *Monty and Ted Riding Across the Plains, Monty and Ted Riding towards the*

Sunset, Who will save these two Innocent men . . .
the list goes on. The actual contents of the
lyrics are amazing, but perhaps enough
embarrassment has been caused.

Two early Morricone-scored Westerns
Duello nel Texas and *Le Pistole non Discutono*
contain examples of lyrics which are not
commensurate with either film content or
musical content. The music to *Le Pistole
non Discutono* is superb. The main title is a
beautiful tune which sensitively conveys
solitary violence through an Allessandroni
whistling solo. The song is beautifully sung
but the lyrics composed by Peter Tevis come
within a totally different musical environment. Consider some of the lines:

Always lonely,
Always looking to get even with the men who did him
    wrong,
That was Billy, Lonesome Billy,
Who was quick to think a gun could make him strong,
No one tougher or more daring, only he and his gun
    sharing,
The great fight to live and his great love to fight,
A rough man who played with danger to whom
    trouble was no stranger,
Until one day he lay dying, he filled his date with
destiny.

Although acceptable Western lyrics, the relationship with the score is oblique. However, despite this, the partnership of this
kind of lyric to the music has created a
strange and unique effect. The violence of
the film, the strength of the score combined
with the impact of the vocal has displaced
what was an intentionally straight lyric
into the realm of black humour. Despite a
mis-match the effect in total has an under-
lying surreal feel which is typical of the
Italian Western. In some cases the mis-
match glares out as pure comic strip
lyricism, but in some cases such as *Le
Pistole non Discutono* other factors create a
strange effect. A similar effect may be seen
in the Don Powell vocal 'Blood Rocks and
Sand' to the Western *And God said to Cain.*
Music was by Carlo Savina.

Danell wrote the lyrics to Morricone's
Duello nel Texas and here we have a straight
example of comic strip mis-match:

**Right and following pages: The Wild Bunch (Valkyries)
sequence from *My Name is Nobody*.**

Keep your hand on your gun,
Don't you trust anyone,
There's only one kind of man you can trust,
That's a dead man, or a gringo like me.
Don't be a fool for a smile or a kiss,
Or your bullet might miss,
Keep your eye on your goal,
There's just one rule that can save you your life,
That's a hand on your knife and the devil in your soul.

As always Morricone's score is superb but the lyric doesn't strictly work. Unfortunately the vein of banal lyrics has run through to many recent Italian Westerns so that in *They Call me Trinity* we are treated to:

He is a sleepy time guy, always takes his time,
But I know you'll be changing your mind,
When you see him use his gun, boy, when you see him use his gun.

The song was a great success in Italy.

We have seen how many Italian Western lyrics parody a violent form of the American lyric:

A Man Must fight to bring Justice back to the land . . . Men will sell their soul for gold . . . A coward gunned him down, I won't rest easy until that coward is found.

Due primarily to the influence of Morricone there was, for a while in Italy, an intense concentration of a typical kind of Western scoring. Soaring trumpet solos accompanied gundowns; cracking whips and bells, shrieks and the choir of Allessandroni could be heard on most scores. In recent years the Italian composer has begun to parody his own unique style. This may be epitomised by the recent Valerii/

Leone film *Il Mio Nome é Nessuno*. The bandits are depicted by a Walkyrie/Good, Bad and Ugly type of musical signature which uses a choir that screams out in imitation of Morricone's previous compositions. Likewise the gundown track contains the sound of a ticking alarm clock *(For a Few Dollars More?)* and a parody on Fonda's theme in *Once Upon a Time in the West*.

In *They Call Me Trinity* Franco Micallizzi's piece 'Al fronte al Killers' contains a fuzzy guitar passage which, combined with the *A Fistful of Dollars* type of percussion, is an obvious retrospective view of the 'sixties Western. Likewise Stelvio Cipriani's scores for the *Alleluja* films and *Blindman*, are too typical of the style that epitomised the typical Italian Western of the 'sixties.

In the American film *Kelly's Heroes* there is a scene when Clint Eastwood confronts a tank. Lalo Schifrin's score echoes the Italian Western gunfight confrontation in a gentle poke at Clint Eastwood.

A closer examination of the types of Italian Western scoring will also reveal moments of non-awareness of self-parody. The unique style had taken such a grip on the Italian composers that they began to parody each other's style – but since we may talk of a 'school of composers' this does not really matter.

Sadly, today, the typical Italian Western score has gone, any revivals are affectionate digs at a style that literally saved the Italian film industry.

Schifrin's score echoes the gunfight confrontation in *Kelly's Heroes* – a gentle poke at Eastwood.

Get it home boys,...I'll get it home'

It has already been argued that the Italian Western has many affiliations, through its amalgam of action and music, to operatic form. It is now necessary to detail the points at which an amalgamation of camera work and soundtrack are utilised to transpose the action into the realm of orchestra-tion, for which the action becomes almost choreographic.

At such points the orchestra takes over the film, and the action of the film becomes a dance of death, the characters play out their roles in subservience to the sound-track. At significant points in the film's

Vision acting through sound-track; still from *Once Upon a Time in the West*.

development, the orchestra comes to the fore and the natural sounds of the film setting are highly diminished or obliterated. The music continues the narration.

Through the development of the Italian Western as a form, a number of stock situations have evolved which command the utilisation of soundtrack in this form. The most significant stock situation to have evolved, is Sergio Leone's 'child' – *La Resa dei Conti,* the gunfight; but this is so important it must be dealt with separately although it should be borne in mind as

the epitome of this technique.

Generally speaking, the orchestra takes over at moments of realisation and reckoning. In the case of Sergio Leone, the moments also include retrospective episodes. In the case of Sergio Sollima and sometimes Sergio Corbucci, the moments are highly choreographic and we have an accompaniment to Cuccillo's desperate flight through the corn fields in *The Big Gundown.* Moments of high tragedy also utilise this technique so that in Corbucci's *The Hellbenders* musical content almost acts as a greek chorus. Moments of confrontation are also highly significant.

The camera work, when used properly, liaises with the orchestra to produce quite dramatic and poignant moments of cinema. One has only to examine the films of Leone and Corbucci to see examples of a successful amalgamation. Examples may be seen time over, of a sweeping camera pan which accompanies significant bars of music. In *Once Upon a Time in the West* during Charles Bronson's final memory sequence of the hanging of his brother, the camera shows a close-up shot of the young Bronson having a harmonica thrust into his mouth by Henry Fonda. Franco de Gemini's brilliant wailing harmonica may be heard in the background. Fonda speaks: 'Keep your loving brother happy . . . play him a tune'. The camera pans back to reveal the entire surrealistic vision of the arch. Morricone's scores sweeps into prominent significance. The camera swings around to survey the solitary ritual through which we may significantly view Monument Valley; cuts to Bronson Jnr.'s face produce a visual moment which acts through soundtrack.

The music can also act as a transcendental medium. It is through Morricone's scoring for Leone that *Once Upon a Time in the West* forces home the point that we are dealing with a microcosmic view of the universe. The music actually acts as an almost mystical corridor, through which we may see the characters play out universal roles. Who could ever forget the power behind the scenes that depict Bronson playing his harmonica to the savagery of 'The man

The graveyard in *The Good, the Bad and the Ugly*.

with the Harmonica' theme. This heightening effect not only lifts the action, but also acts as a form of grand commentary.

At such moments, the action of the film ceases to be as important as the position that the music has commandeered. In *The Good, the Bad and the Ugly* there is a scene in which Tuco rushes frantically around the circular graveyard to find the grave of Arch Stanton, the grave in which the gold is supposed to be buried. Morricone accompanies his frantic search with a piece of music called 'The Ecstasy of Gold'. The term Ecstasy accurately describes the heights to which we are taken. In *The Mercenary* there is a piece of music entitled 'The Ecstasy of Violence'. The music becomes an ecstatic aural interpretation of situation, the grand orchestra provides a grand *operatic* commentary on the action and *becomes* action. . . .

This method of writing film music epitomises the role of film music composer as director. It is not surprising that Leone often directs with Morricone's music playing over the speaker system whilst on location, not merely added on to the soundtrack after shooting. The opera (from the production point of view) requires the careful attention of both musical director and director for the movement, choreography, or whatever. In the Italian Western the role of the film composer is exactly the same.

Many Italian Western scores are often moulded in an almost operatic classical mould. A composer whose scores are very much of this ilk is Carlo Rustichelli. Highly classical orchestration skilfully combined with the action, produces some startling effects quite unique to the Western genre. In *The Riders of Vengeance* and *The Man, the Pride and the Vengeance* a highly classical arrangement brought the whole of the action on to a profound and serious level. In *God Forgives, I Don't* a very brutal Western, (banned in Australia), Rustichelli included a parody on the Dies Irae in a score which was a mixture of straight classical and pure Western.

The Italian Western's Operatic Vision

manifests itself at moments of realisation and reckoning. We might roughly categorise these into three sections: *La Resa dei Conti,* Pure Tragedy, and a final section which might be split between confrontation and choreography.

In discussing the musical accompani-

nent to gunfights we are embarking upon a large area which is deserving of a closer examination. Gunfights in the Italian Western often act as points at which the symbols of the story reconcile themselves. For Leone the gunfight closes the circle of life and death, a very old classical concept as well as a feature of operatic symbolism. The gunfight in all of Leone's Westerns takes place in a circle: The circular coral in *Once Upon a Time in the West*, graveyard in *The Good, the Bad and the Ugly*, circle of stones in *For a Few Dollars More* and the architectural surrounds of *A Fistful of*

In *God Forgives, I Don't*, the *Dies Irae* accompanies the riding of the Wild Bunch.

From *The Hellbenders* – cosmological tragedy to the emotive power of music.

Dollars. The circle is a physical symbol of cosmological action – this action is sealed through vision – in turn supplied by the score. The settling of accounts and tying of threads is achieved through music; why else would the watch and Harmonica be so important to Leone? The meeting of symbols is both actual and musical.

The second section takes account of pure tragedy. At such moments the score performs a grandiose function. That is to say that the pure power, energy and emotional content of the music is such as to provide emotional reaction through an aural stimulus.

In the concluding scene of *The Hellbenders* we are confronted with a highly tragic situation, very close to that of Greek Tragedy. The entire family is almost obliterated, the three brothers having shot each other through greed – the third and youngest being a victim of the situation; the girl is dying of pneumonia and Joseph Cotten is also dying of a bullet wound. Moved by absolute despair Cotten insanely crawls across the mud flats by the river to float the flag of the Hellbenders across the water. As he pathetically crawls across the flats Morricone's score commences a final tragic salute. The score echoes the sound of a dying Southern Army bugle call. Combined with incredible emotive power and the remarkable voice of Edda Dell'Orso a piece of music may be heard which acts as a superb commentary on the entire tragedy. The sheer power of the score combined with Corbucci's direction of a scene of pure desolation, demonstrates how the Italian Western often produces a cosmological vision.

In Leone's *Once Upon a Time in the West* during the scene in which Jill initially travels to Sweetwater after disembarking from the train, we hear the first strains of 'Jill's theme' on the soundtrack. As the cart is driven across the plains, with suitable shots of Monument Valley, Morricone's score acts on two levels. On one level it is a salute to the West which is passing, signified by Monument Valley, on another level it is a sad accompaniment to the fore knowledge

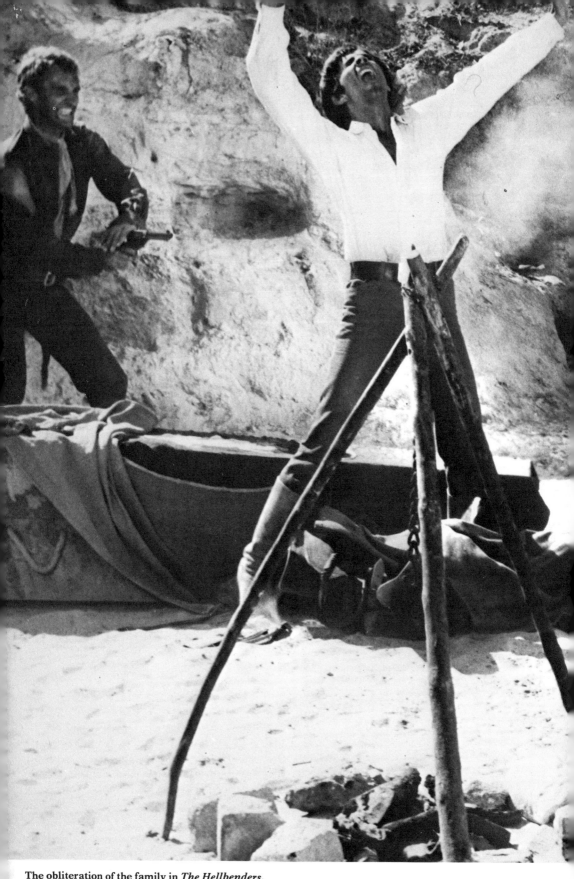

The obliteration of the family in *The Hellbenders*.

which we possess regarding the shooting of the McBain family. As Jill is driven across the valley the camera pans back to reveal a Dali-esque depiction of the West, the suitably emotive voice of Edda Dell'Orso completes the moment.

Emotive music as commentary, may always be found in film, but in *Duck You Sucker* as in *West* the music seems to exclude all else in moments of high tragedy. In the scene in which Rod Steiger (Juan) returns to find his family massacred the camera inquisitively follows his view as he surveys the scene to the arrangement of the *figli*

morti composition. This kind of accompaniment was also used in *The Grand Silence* when an arrangement of violins and suitable percussion visualised the desolation, loneliness and tragedy of the white landscape. Moments of real pathos were conveyed by the sole use of Morricone's score.

John Phillip Law rescued in *Death Rides a Horse*.

This kind of highly emotive use of music may be traced throughout the Italian Cinema of the sixties and seventies but perhaps particularly so in, and perhaps even because of, the Italian Western. In *The Man, the Pride and the Vengeance* and *Fort Yuma Gold* dramatic crescendoes of power convey desolation at suitable, poignant moments. Rustichelli's classical scoring really transcends the scene to catch the genre and bring it onto almost classical levels. The 'Death of Antony' score is such a moment of release.

The final category can be divided into confrontation and choreography. Confrontation taken to its natural conclusion is manifest in the gunfight, but there are plenty of other moments of realisation in the Italian Western. In the film *Sabata,* Giombini wrote a slow powerful piece entitled 'Nel Covo di Stengel', which can be heard when Lee Van Cleef first encounters the villain Stengel in his study. As Van Cleef (Sabata) enters, the score almost painfully traces Van Cleef's survey of the lair. Similarly in *Quien Sabe* the theme salutes Beswick's confrontation with Volonté.

Music used as choreography can be epitomised by Sollima's *The Big Gundown*. Morricone composed a special treatment of shrill flutes and voices to depict Cucillo's plight and flight across the landscape. In the cornfield scene, heavy percussion is added to produce an almost choreographic sequence. This kind of combination of music and action may be seen in *Five Man Army* – the running of the Japanese; *Death Rides a Horse* – Van Cleef's journey across the terrain; and perhaps memorably so in *For a Few Dollars More* in the scenes where Volonté's band ride across horizonal peaks in time to 'The Vice of Killing'.

It can certainly be said that the whole genre verges on the surreal, when what is in essence a vision becomes so closely choreographed. The unique blend of scoring and action in *Rainbow* acts as a symbolic landscape for which the music speaks as much, if not at times more, than the action itself.

'Only at the point of death'

The musical apex of the Italian Western; still from *Once Upon a Time in the West*.

In *Once Upon a Time in the West* Harmonica's reply to Frank's question as to who he is, is that he will reveal all only at the point of death. Frank significantly replies 'I know'. The pair then retreat to Leone's obsessive circular corral for the gunfight. The moment has arrived for the settling of accounts; it is not only a natural conclusion to the encounter, it is also the point of natural evolution of the film. Frank realises, as do we, that the gunfight *must* take place — *La Resa dei Conti* has arrived. It is at the moment of the gunfight that we reach the apex of the Italian Western, this feature above all else characterises the Italian style of Western. But more than the mere fact

Ennio Morricone.

of the gunfight, it is also the music which accompanies these encounters that is the true mark of the genre. Some mention has already been made of *La Resa dei Conti* and now we must elaborate. The term comes from the magnificent piece of Morricone-composed music which accompanies the *For a Few Dollars More* gunfight sequence between Van Cleef and Gian-Maria Volonté. I apply the term to the significant gunfight that takes place in most Italian Westerns.

It seems almost certain that the convention is attributable to Sergio Leone and Ennio Morricone. A suggestion of the form was made in *A Fistful of Dollars* when the final gunfight between Clint Eastwood and Gian-

Leone presents us with camera shots of the protagonist's hand, hovering above the holster, to the accompaniment of a percussive echo – a trademark of Morricone.

Maria Volonté took place accompanied by a trumpet solo from Michele Lacerenza entitled 'Per Un Pugno Di Dollari' but retitled 'The Man with No Name' in the States and Great Britain. The pair waited to draw, whilst the music played, but Leone did not make full use of the musical encounter as he was to in his later films. The music was an accompaniment, in his later films it became an integral feature.

La Resa dei Conti is significant for a number of reasons. In Leone it performs a symbolic function, a conclusion of the cycle of life and death. It ties up the threads of the encounter and musically it gives the film's music composer the opportunity to really 'come to the fore' in what is the grand finale piece, as in grand death scenes in the opera. These moments of encounter become so intense that they are an almost ecstatic experience. In *For a Few Dollars More* the intensity of the gunfight came close to 'religious experience'. This was no mere 'encounter at the OK Corral à-la-Americano' – the Volonté character is a mass of passionate psychological states and obsessions brilliantly suggested by Morricone's music.

The *Resa dei Conti* convention was copied by almost every Italian director after Leone. In this connection, three directors should be discussed individually: Sergio Leone, Sergio Sollima and Sergio Corbucci. In the work of all these three composers examples can be seen of a specific form of the *Resa dei Conti* convention in operation.

Sergio Leone may be regarded as the effectual father of the form. In *A Fistful of Dollars* Michele Lacerenza's trumpet solo accompanied the gunfight between Eastwood and Volonté – but *not* the draw. Although poignantly present, the music was a subdued melody to an obsessive percussive beat of the form that was to be repeated in *The Hellbenders* – the theme was present but was not what we may term ecstatic. It was in *For a Few Dollars More* that an intense collaboration with Morricone produced a gunfight theme which acted on a metaphysical level. In the opening bars of the theme, the strains of a church organ can be

Neo-Beethoven accompanies the gunfight in *The Big Gundown*.

heard, bringing to mind the quasi-religious undertones. The musical watch melody combined with a frenetic Spanish guitar piece, prepare the audience for the encounter. In the film Eastwood says 'Now we start . . .' and the strains of a powerful, no longer subdued, trumpet solo prepare for the dramatic encounter. A similar kind of formula was adopted in *The Good, the Bad and the Ugly* when a percussion-accompanied Spanish guitar solo was heard during the triple gundown between Wallach, Eastwood and Van Cleef. In the actual film in cinematic terms the effect was remarkable. Leone presented us with camera shots of the protagonists' hands hovering above their holsters to the sound of a percussive echo, a trade mark of Morricone.

In the cinema of Sergio Leone the gun-fight is metaphysical, and in the work of Corbucci and Sollima the music takes the form of commentary, but very much in the Leone idiom.

The gundown motif may be prominently seen in three of Sollima's films: *The Big Gundown, Run Man Run* and *Face to Face*. Morricone scored *Gundown* and *Face*. In *The Big Gundown* Cucillo has three musical encounters. One melody is neo-Beethoven and one of the others has the familiar trumpet strains, although rather more military than soaring in style. Each piece accompanies Cucillo's draw with his knife. The music produces a tense and dramatic effect but we are clearly not dealing with a Leone.

Bruno Nicolai, whose compositions are not dissimilar to those of Ennio Morricone, scored *Run Man Run* which also featured Cucillo. Likewise, the duel sequences feature a trumpet solo and the power and energy is very reminiscent of *The Big Gundown* score.

In *Face to Face* we are back with the power of Morricone. In this film the grand gun-fight occurs mid-film, with no shoot-out actually taking place, due to the removal of one of the protagonists' bullets. The score is a pounding, obsessive piece with organ and trumpet in true Morricone style, tension mounts and again the scene successfully transcends itself.

Corbucci's use of Morricone's gunfight scoring is unlike Leone's and Sollima's since the music acts as background as opposed to involvement. A fuzzy guitar version of the theme 'The Penguin' may be heard in *Compañeros,* but no tension mounts between the confrontation of Nero and Tomas Milian, Corbucci is merely playing out a convention. In *A Professional Gun* we almost seem to have returned to Leone's circular motif since the final shoot-out between Jack Palance and Tony Musante (Eufemio) is in the centre of a circular bull ring. In this confrontation there is power, the score is magnificent and more Morricone than Morricone; staccato echoing percussion, guitar and soaring trumpet all com-

In *Once Upon a Time in the West* the same kind of idea adopted in *For a Few Dollars More* was repeated, with Bronson's Harmonica becoming the feature of the gun-fight piece. After a few minutes of Franco De Gemini's brilliant playing there are the savage guitar chords that identify with Henry Fonda. The composition was a masterpiece – it was this theme that really made a name for Ennio Morricone on the

'The Penguin', in *Compañeros*.

bine to sum up the Italian Western gunfight form. Camera shots switch between Palance and Musante under the surveillance of Franco Nero in very much a *For a Few Dollars More* fashion.

Morricone's convention of trumpet solo with gunfight brought about a surge of trumpet/gunfight composition for most of the Italian Westerns. In *Dead Men Ride (Anda Muchancho Spara)* the protagonist breaks open a bag of gold . . . When the bag is empty 'We shoot'; to the flowing of the gold we hear a dramatic and magnificent trumpet composition by Bruno Nicolai. All very much reminiscent of *For a Few Dollars More* — right down to the memory sequence. Michele Lacerenza, the trumpet player on *A Fistful of Dollars,* began to compose his own film scores and did a very good job for *L'Ira di Dio (The Wrath of God)*. The gunfight composition was released as a single on the Cam label 'Concerto for a Killer'. A combination of classical piano and trumpet really ensured the prominent position of composition in encounter sequences. The number of trumpet gunfight sequences are endless: Nino Rosso the internationally famous trumpet player came forth with 'Yankee', Nico Fidenco featured trumpet quite often in his scoring, for example 'Bury them Deep' (complete with Allessandroni chanting), 'Uno Dopo L'Altro', a highly classical arrangement, 'God Said to Cain'; De Masi's 'Thousand Dollars on The Red'. On occasions the gunfight sequence would vary: in *Death Rides a Horse* there is a ritualistic chanting which crescendoes and culminates at the point of the draw (Morricone). In *Revenge at El Paso* the Rustichelli score accompanies the gunfight while a roulette wheel is spinning. The music is a waltz supposedly being played by the Hotel Orchestra.

The *Resa dei Conti* feature of the Italian Western can be seen to have been exceptionally important. From a convention, a large number of records were produced, and an individuality brought to a genre which was to be known derogatorily as the *Spaghetti Western.*

I Maestri-Personalities in Western Composing

(a) Gianni Ferrio

Gianni Ferrio was born in Vicenza in 1924, where he subsequently studied music. His original intention was to study medicine, but it did not take him long to realise that music was the prime love of his life. In his early career he composed songs for Teddy Reno and also made some radio transmissions. He really began to compose for the cinema in 1960. Unlike several other film composers Ferrio cannot really be regarded as part of the repertory system. Ferrio has not figured in many other musicians' orchestras or output. His style of composition is highly original and his particular use of percussion, guitar and soft wind instruments has enabled him to cultivate a highly effective and original form of composition. In 1968 he joined forces with Ennio Morricone to write the score for *Fort Yuma Gold* which although substantially Ferrio's music has some Morricone themes.

Western film compositions include: *Kings of the West, The Texas Twins, One Silver Dollar, Fort Yuma Gold, The Most Vicious Bandit in the West, Wanted, Find a Place to Die, Alive is better than Dead, Los Desperados, A Man called Sledge, Vengeance is Mine, El Desperado, Djurado, Death Sentence, They call me Requiescat* and many others.

(b) Benedetto Ghiglia

Ghiglia was a native of Florence and brought up in a highly artistic environment. His father Oscar Ghiglia was a classical guitarist of international fame. Until about 1969 Ghiglia was a very active composer for the cinema, but has since turned to his own individual work. His style is also very individual bearing a rather shallow sound of driving percussion and electric guitar. His score for *A Dollar in the Teeth* although not really Morricone's style is an amalgam of everything typically Italian Western, cracking whips, fuzzy guitar, bells and cracking rifle-butts. He has not produced many scores for the Italian Western, but what has been produced is original and significant.

Western film compositions: *Adios Gringo, A Dollar in the Teeth, El Rojo* and *Starblack.*

(c) Luis Enriquez Bacalov

Bacalov is probably the odd man out in our gallery of Western film composers, because, although he has been heavily identified with Italian film scoring, he is, in fact, of Spanish origin. Bacalov has, however, worked and lived for most of his life in Italy and his close association with many prominent Italian film composers, has resulted in the development of a unique Italian style.

Bacalov started his career by working both with Allessandro Allessandroni and Ennio Morricone. In the early 1960s Bacalov formed a group entitled 'Luis Enriquez and His Electronic Men'; this was a group based loosely upon the English equivalent, 'The Tornadoes', who rocketed to the top of the English charts with a record called 'Telstar'. One of the Group's prominent guitarists often signed the name De Mutis to some of the Group's compositions – this guitarist was Allessandro Allessandroni who chose to use his wife's maiden name as a *nom de plume*. Bacalov was essentially a pianist with many famous Italian composers and eventually formed his own orchestra. Much of his composition has a definite Morricone influence, which probably stems from the Italian repertory system of composition. Morricone supervised the music to the film *A Bullet for the*

General which was composed by Bacalov.

Some of Bacalov's compositions for the Italian Western include: *A Bullet for The General, Django, The Price of Power, Sugar Colt, The Greatest Kidnapping in the West, The Land of My Father.*

(d) Riz Ortolani

Riz Ortolani was born in 1926 of a large family of musicians. He was born in Pesaro and obtained his qualification in music at the City Conservatorio of Pesaro.

Ortolani came to world-wide recognition with his composition for the film *Mondo Cane,* one of the feature titles being the award-winning song 'More'. Ortolani has his own highly original approach to composition, which consists basically of the lush use of strings. One has only to listen to the music of the film *The Yellow Rolls-Royce* and compare it with *Mondo Cane* to realize that there is just as much indimitable stamp to his style as there is to the music of Ennio Morricone. Unfortunately, the romantic approach of Ortolani's music does not always complement the savagery of the Italian Western. For example, the score for the film *Beyond the Law* fails miserably, but on the other hand the harsher treatment of *Day of Anger* achieves moments of operatic encounter.

Some of the films for which he has composed include: *Night of the Serpent, Beyond the Law, Day of Anger, Apaches Last Battle, Gun Fight at High Noon, Let Them Rest, Ride and Kill* and *Seven from Texas.*

(e) Nico Fidenco

Nico Fidenco started his career as a popular singer. Today he is an acknowledged composer of music for film. Fidenco often worked with Allessandro Allessandroni and the Cantori Moderni and consequently with the repertory system of composition in Italy; some of the influence of Allessandro Allessandroni, possibly through Ennio Morricone, has permeated his compositions. Many established Italian Western music conventions may be seen in his work: for example, he often uses a soaring trumpet solo for gun fights and for certain solit-

ary moments. In his score 'John the Bastard' Allessandroni's familiar *Fistful-of-Dollars* chanting can be prominently heard on many tracks. Grunting, whips and bells again form the panoramic background for his composition. He has even used the unique voice of Gianna Spagnolo.

Fidenco's compositions are unquestionably original, and with the passing of an era, Fidenco may certainly be regarded as a milestone in the music of the Italian Western cinema. Almost without exception, Fidenco has scored either Western or Adventure films and we look forward to following his future development as a composer of music for the cinema.

Films for which he has composed include: *Ringo the Texican, John the Bastard, I Want Him Dead, In the Shadow of a Colt, To Hell and Back, All'Ultimo Sangue.*

(f) Carlo Rustichelli

Rustichelli was a native of Carpi (Modena) and was born there in 1916. He obtained a diploma in pianoforte at Bologna, and a diploma in composition from Rome. Rustichelli has worked with the cinema since 1942 and, consequently, has a particularly original and established style. His style is predominantly classically orientated. Most of his scoring for Western films has either had a very strong epic feel, as in the superb *The Riders of Vengeance,* or his Western scores have a strange Italian romantic feel (in the folk sense) as in *Boot Hill* or *Revenge at El Paso.*

His Italian scores include: *Two Guns for a Coward, Train to Durango, Night of the Desperado, Kill or be Killed, I Go, I See, I Shoot, Revenge at El Paso, Dead or Alive, Buffalo Bill – Hero of the Far West, Boot Hill, Blood River, God Forgives I Don't, The Riders of Vengeance.*

(g) Francesco de Masi

Francesco de Masi was born in 1930 in Rome. He studied composition at San Pietro a Maiella in Naples. De Masi has written for the cinema quite prolifically since the 1960s and is very interested in classical orchestration. His compositions for the Italian Western are identifiable by a prominent use of harpsichord, electric bass and electric guitar. De Masi's style is instantly recognizable as being Italian comic strip, in the same way that we might regard Dimitri Tiomkin and Frankie Lane as being American comic strip. We seldom encounter the operatic feel for the grandiose in De Masi's scores as we might in Rustichelli's or Morricone's, but his contribution to the Italian Western has been immense.

Western films for which he has scored include: *For a Fist in the Eye, Seven Dollars on the Red, The Cost of Dying, Two Gun Men, Ringo the Face of Revenge, Ranch of the Ruthless, The Moment to Kill, Kill Them all and Come Back Alive, I'll Go, I'll Kill Him and Come Back, The Pitiless Colt of the Gringo, Fifteen Scaffolds for a Killer, The Dirty Story of the West,* and the famous *Arizona Colt.*

(h) Stelvio Cipriani

Stelvio Cipriani was born in Rome and obtained his diploma at the Conservatorio di Santa Cecilia. In his early years he directed the orchestra for the famous Italian pop singer Rita Pavone. Most of his time, however, has been spent in film scoring and in working with popular music. He has even been commissioned to write for Orson Welles on NBC. Cipriani lived for some time in New York where he was a good friend of Dave Brubeck. Much of Cipriani's music, whilst being original, also contains many Italian Western musical conventions: for example, trumpet solos for gun fights, choral grunts and groans with electric guitar work. The score to the film *Blind Man* uses a piercing cry in the same way as Allessandroni's cry was used in *The Good, the Bad and the Ugly.* It is fair to say that in much of Cipriani's composition there may be seen quite definite influences of the Italian repertory system, in other words, Cipriani belongs to the Morricone, Nicolai, Fidenco, Allessandroni school.

Films for which he has composed include, among others: *Heads You Die Tails I Kill You, They Call Him Alleluia, The Return of Alleluia, Blind Man, The Bounty Killer, A Man, a Horse and a Gun, Nevada.*

(i) Bruno Nicolai

The name Bruno Nicolai has been linked with that of Ennio Morricone in a number of different ways. For several years many people outside of Italy were under the distinct impression that Ennio Morricone and Bruno Nicolai were one and the same person. The main reason for this being that there is a definite similarity between their style of composition. Whilst it was quite easy to obtain photographs and information concerning the biography of Ennio Morricone, it is rather curious that there have been very few photographs and little available biographical information about Bruno Nicolai.

Apart from Ennio Morricone, Bruno Nicolai is certainly the most important name in the Italian cinema from the film music aspect. Yet, curiously, this great composer and musician has remained in an eclipse.

Bruno Nicolai was trained in the Roman school of Goffredo Petrassi. Nicolai's musical career has run parallel with Morricone's and, not only have they composed together, but Nicolai has also conducted the majority of Morricone's work. It is difficult to regard the two as being separate. Bruno Nicolai experiments with composition in very much the same way as Morricone does. Both seem to share a similar logic of progression in composition. Nicolai's musical dialogue for the cinema works on the same kind of relationship as does Morricone's. The point which should perhaps be considered is how individual is he as a composer and how has this contradiction occurred. Amongst Nicolai's compositions may be found music which is distinctly original, and distinctly also, the work of a man isolated from the influence of the Italian repertory system. The music for *Una Giornata Spesa Bene* and the Western *Corri Uomo Corri* is original, but the music to *The Land Raiders* and *Indio Black* is undeniably in the style of Ennio Morricone. Morricone said, when being interviewed in Rome, that he does not listen to other composers nor go to the cinema for fear of being influenced. It has also been said that Nicolai has, on occasion, been especially asked to compose in a Morricone style. One may conclude that, through his extremely close association with Morricone's music and musicians, a degree of influence has permeated Nicolai's work, and Nicolai himself is probably aware of this.

Bruno Nicolai is a very great composer – there can be no mistake about this, and the relationship that he has with Ennio Morricone is unique. His music for the Italian Western has created greater depths in the action.

Very few of his records are easily obtainable – most of his output being privately published by his own company, Gemelli.

His works for the Western include: *A Professional Gun* (with Morricone), *The Land Raiders*, *El Cisco*, *Django Shoots First*, *Days of Violence*, *The Challenge of The McKennas*, *Indio Black*, *Dead Men Ride*, *A Man Called Apocalypse Joe*, *Run Man Run*, *A Thousand Dollars For Ringo*, *A Man Called Shanghai Joe*.

(j) Allessandro Allessandroni

Allessandro Allessandroni has only written the music for one Western, and that was written specifically after the style of Morricone. His importance, however, to not only the Italian Western, but the Italian cinema as a whole, is tremendous and, therefore, must be included in this chapter.

Allessandroni was born in Rome in 1925. He studied at the University of Economics and, ironically, has never had a formal musical training. His development in the world of music has grown purely out of interest. In the early days of his musical career he toured night-clubs in Germany singing and playing the piano. When he returned to Italy, he formed a quartet after the style of The Four Freshmen entitled The Four Caravels. The female member of The Four Caravels was his wife, and one of the other members was Guido Cincerelli, who is now in charge of film sound-tracks at RCA in Rome.

Allessandroni had had a close association and friendship with Ennio Morricone from the time that they were both boys. Therefore, when Morricone was asked to compose music for the film *A Fistful of Dollars*, it was Allessandroni who not only played the guitar and whistled on the sound-track, but The Four Caravels were enlarged, at Morricone's suggestion, to the distinct and original sound of the Cantori Moderni. From this point, Allessandroni's fame and reputation grew, as did the size of the Cantori Moderni to the now established twelve or sixteen members.

Allessandroni and his choir have made a singular contribution to the world of the Italian Western, since the solitary, lonely whistle that is often heard on Italian Western sound-tracks, is the whistle of Allessandroni, and the unique choral accompaniment will almost certainly be that of the Cantori Moderni. It may well be true to say that in a partnership of this kind, the individual sound of people such as Morricone, Cipriani and Fidenco to a large extent stems from this man. To appreciate a really fine example of Allessandroni's accomplishments in choral arranging listen to the sound-track of *Navajo Joe*.

Allessandroni now spends a considerable amount of his time composing, and one can look forward to the future development of another very fine and original Italian composer.

(k) Ennio Morricone

Ennio Morricone is a native of Rome and was born in 1928. He obtained a diploma in trumpet, composition, musical direction and choral work at the Conservatorio di Santa Cecilia. He studied composition, as did Bruno Nicolai, with Goffredo Petrassi. He initially studied and worked in the field of what is popularly known as serious music, and few people are aware that he has not only composed music for a ballet, *Requiem For Destiny*, but also quartets, concertos and many diverse kinds of symphonic composition. His composition 'Suoni Per Dino' was in the finals of the Festival of Contemporary Music at Venice in 1969.

Although Morricone had composed the music for the film *Gun Fight at Red Sands* before the appearance of *A Fistful of Dollars*, it was essentially the music for Leone's first film that marked the commencement of his career as a film composer. It has been said that, to a large extent, Morricone *is* the Italian Western. He would seem to have a capacity for creating an entirely new dialogue between music and cine film. This dialogue works so well that a Morricone score can heighten and create new dimensions to a film. His unique sound, which in many Westerns involves a startling use of percussion and chorus has not only led to many imitations, but has also come to be identified as a major part of the essence of Italian Western cinema.

It is only of recent years that the public have started to realise that there is far more to Morricone than merely Western composition. The sheer volume of his musical output verges on the unbelievable (and it is consistently very good). His composition for many other cinematic genres has also been brilliant and his more serious compositions, such as 'Ecce Homo' and 'A Quiet Place in the Country' realise great heights of achievement in composition.

His music is so overwhelming that it is difficult to write about and must really be heard. There is little doubt, however, that Morricone has the makings of genius.

Italian Westerns for which he has written include: *Gun Fight at Red Sands, A Fistful of Dollars, For a Few Dollars More, The Good, the Bad and the Ugly, Once Upon a Time in the West, Duck You Sucker, Face to Face, A Pistol for Ringo, Return of Ringo, The Big Gundown, A Professional Gun, Tepepa, The J & S Band, Compañeros, Life's Tough Isn't It, Ah Well that's Providence, Bullets Don't Argue, The Hellbenders, The Grand Silence, A Roof for a Skyful of Stars, What Am I Doing in the Revolution, Seven Guns for the McGregors, Seven Brides for the McGregors, Navajo Joe, The Hills Run Red, Fort Yuma Gold, Five Man Army, Death Rides a Horse, Bullet for the General.*

Pseudonyms under which Morricone has scored: Leo Nichols, Dan Savio.

(l) Other Important Figures

Finally, mention must be made of certain key personalities in Italian Western composition to whom a separate section has not been devoted here. The female voice which may be heard on the sound-track to *Once Upon a Time in the West* and *Face to Face* is that of a young lady named Edda Dell'Orso. The voice of Edda is a unique aural ex-perience and is an important factor in the creation of mood in Italian sound-track. Likewise, the individual voice of Gianna Spagnolo has been effectively used by composers such as Morricone and Fidenco to create a markedly individual Italian Western *Italian* sound. Spagnolo's voice on the sound track to *The Hills Run Red* gives a certain earthiness to the music. Morricone is renowned for surrounding himself with musicians of very high standard, and mention must be made of the contribution of Franco de Gemini's harmonica which creates an almost metaphysical dimension under Morricone direction. The trumpet playing of Michele Lacerenza, who has also scored several Italian Westerns (e.g. *The Anger of God*) and who plays trumpet in *A Fistful of Dollars,* is also deserving of note.

There are many other composers to whom a section has not been allotted who must, therefore, here be given credit: Angelo Lavagnino, Marcello Giombini, Lalo Gori, and Nora Orlandi, have all contributed greatly to creating the individual flavour of the Italian Western.

FILMOGRAPHY

This is a representative list of Italian Westerns released in England since 1965. For reasons of space and lack of further information it has proved impossible to list all Italian Westerns made from the sixties onwards. For further information the reader is recommended to consult the check-list of David Austen in his article *Continental Westerns, Films and Filming*, Vol. 17, No. 10, July 1971, pp. 36-44, and *Monthly Film Bulletin*. Another source is *Der Italo Western*, a catalogue compiled in 1969 by Alice Goetz and Helmut W. Banz, published by the *Verband der Deutschen Filmclubs*. The check-lists, published in *Monthly Film Bulletin* of Jan. 1967, pp. 18-19; Feb. 1969, p. 43 and Nov. 1971, p. 231, will be another aid to the reader in finding his way through the maze of pseudonyms used in the Italian film industry. Finally, the books published annually by Unitalia Film are of great value in providing lists and further details of Italian Westerns, many of which have not been released here.

The following list is compiled in alphabetical order, from the date of the film release in this country. Where a different release title from that originally given exists, the film will be found under the British title. The abbreviations are: *Asst. d:* Assistant director, *D:* Director, *M:* Music, *Md:* Musical direction, *P:* Producer, *Sc:* Script, *Ph:* Photography, *Lp:* Leading players, *alt. It. title:* alternative Italian title, *Fr:* France, *It:* Italy, *Sp:* Spain, *W. Germ.:* West Germany.

Also listed are the British distribution companies at the time of the film's release, as well as the British Board of Film Censor's certificate categories of U, A, AA, and X. Where numbers are found in brackets, alongside the numbers denoting the running time of a film at release, the original running time before cuts is referred to.

1965

Buffalo Bill, Hero of the Far West (Buffalo Bill, L'Eroe del Far West). *It, W. Germ, Fr.* 1964.
Eagle. U.
P: Solly Bianco. *D:* John W. Fordson (Mario Costa).
Sc: Nino Stresso, Luciano Martino, from a story by Nino Stresso. *Ph:* Jack Dalmas (Massimo Dallamano). *M:* Carlo Rustichelli. *Md:* Franco Ferraro. 93 mins.
Lp: Gordon Scott, Jan Hendriks, Mario Brega.

Duel at Rio Bravo (Jennie Lees ha una nuova pistola).
It, Sp, Fr. 1964.
Compton Cameo. U.
D: Tullio Demichelli. *Sc:* Gene Linotto.
Ph: M. A. Capriotti. *M, Md:* Angelo Francesco Lavagnino. 90 (100) mins.
Lp: Guy Madison, Madeleine Lebeau, Fernando Sancho.

The Magnificent Three (Tres Hombres Buenos, *alt. It. title:* I Tre Implacabili). *Sp, It.* 1963.
Compton Cameo. U.
D: Joaquin L. Romero Marchent. *Sc:* José Mallorqui (Mario Caiano). *Ph:* Rafael Pacheco. *M:* Manuel Paroda, Francesco de Masi. 69 mins.
Lp: Geoffrey Horne, Robert Hundar, Fernando Sancho.

Ride and Kill (Cavalco e Uccidi). *It, Sp.* 1963.
Compton Cameo. U.
D: J. L. Boraw. *Sc:* J. Mallorqui (Mario Caiano).
Ph: Aldo Greci, Mario Sbrenna. *M:* Riz Ortolani. 70 mins.
Lp: Alex Nicol, Margaret Grayson, Robert Hundar.

1966

Gun Fight at High Noon (El Sabor de la Vengenza, *alt. It. title:* I Tre Spietati). *Sp, It.* 1963.
Compton Cameo. U.

D: J. L. Romero Marchent. *Sc:* Jesus Navarro, J. H. Marchent, Rafael Romero Marchent. *Ph:* Rafael Pacheco. *M:* Riz Ortolani. 88 mins.
Lp: Richard Harrison, Robert Hundar, Gloria Milland, Fernando Sancho.

A Pistol for Ringo (Una Pistola per Ringo). *It, Sp.* 1965. Miracle. A.
P: Luciano Ercoli, Albert Pugliese. *D:* Duccio Tessari. *Ph:* Francesco Marin. *M:* Ennio Morricone. 99 mins.
Lp: Montgomery Wood (Giuliano Gemma), Hally Hammond (Lorella de Luca), Fernando Sancho, Antonio Casas, Nièves Navarro.

Seven Hours of Gunfire (Adventuras del Oeste). *Sp, It, W. Germ.* 1964.
D: J. L. Romero Marchent. *Ph:* Rafael Pacheco. *M, Md:* Angelo Francesco Lavagnino. 89 (96) mins.
Lp: Clyde Rogers (Rick van Nutter), Elga Sommefueld, Adrian Hoven.

Shoot First, Laugh Last (Un Uomo, un Cavallo, Una Pistola). *It, W. Germ, USA.* 1967. Amanda. X.
P: Roberto Infascelli, Massimo Gualdi. *Executive P:* Allen Klein. *Sc:* José Many (Giuseppe Mangione), Bob Enescelle Jnr. from a story by Tony Antony. *Ph:* Marcello Masciocchi. *M:* Stelvio Cipriani. 79 (90) mins.
Lp: Tony Antony, Dan Vadis, Marco Gugliemi.

They Call Me Trinity (Lo Chiamanvano Trinità). *It.* 1970. Avco Embassy. A.
P: Italo Zingarelli *D:* E. B. Clucher (Enzo Barboni). *Sc:* E. B. Clucher. *Ph:* Aldo Giordani. *M:* Franco Micalizzi. 93 (100) mins.
Lp: Terence Hill, Bud Spencer, Farley Granger.

1967
Adios Gringo. *It, Sp, Fr.* 165.
Golden Era. X.
P: Bruno Turchetto. *D:* George Finlay (Giorgio Stegani). *Ph:* Francisco Sempere. *M:* Benedetto Ghiglia. 98 mins.
Lp: Giuliano Gemma, Evelyn Stewart (Ida Galli), Roberto Camardiel.

A Fistful of Dollars (Per un Pugno di Dollari). *It, W. Germ, Sp.* 1964.
United Artists. X.

P: Harry Colombo (Arrigo Colombo), George Papi (Giorgio Papi). *D:* Sergio Leone. *Sc:* Sergio Leone, Duccio Tessari. *Ph:* Jack Dalmas (Massimo Dallamano). *M:* Dan Savio (Ennio Morricone). 95 (100) mins.
Lp: Clint Eastwood, Marianne Koch, John Wells (Gian-Maria Volonté).

For a Few Dollars More (Per Qualche Dollari in Piu). *It, W. Germ.* 1965.
United Artists. X.
P: Alberto Grimaldi. *D:* Sergio Leone. *Asst. d:* Tonino Valerii. *Sc:* Sergio Leone, Luciano Vincenzoni. *Ph:* Massimo Dallamano. *M:* Ennio Morricone. 128 (130) mins.
Lp: Clint Eastwood, Lee Van Cleef, Gian-Maria Volonté, Klaus Kinsky, Mario Brega.

The Hills Run Red (Un Fiume di Dollari). *It.* 1966.
United Artists. A.
P: Dino de Laurentis. *D:* Lee W. Beaver (Carlo Lizzani). *Sc:* Mario Pierotti. *Ph:* Antonio Secchi. *M:* Leo Nichols (Ennio Morricone). 89 mins.
Lp: Thomas Hunter, Henry Silva, Dan Duryea, Nando Gazzolo, Nicoletta Machiavelli.

In a Colt's Shadow (All' Ombra di una Colt). *It, Sp.* 1965.
Warner Pathé. U.
P: Vincenzo Genesi. *D:* Gianni Grimaldi. *Ph:* Julio Ortas, Stelvio Massi. *M:* Nico Fidenco. 68 (85) mins.
Lp: Stephen Forsyth, Conrado Sanmartin.

Killer's Canyon (Jim Il Primo). *It.* 1964.
British Lion. U.
D: Serge Bergen (Sergio Berganzelli). *Ph:* Amerigo Gengarelli. *M:* Marsello Gigante. 96 (98) mins.
Lp: Cameron Mitchell, Carl Möhner, Celina Cely.

Minnesota Clay. *It, Sp, Fr.* 1964.
Compton Cameo. A.
P: Danilo Marciani. *D:* Sergio Corbucci. *Ph:* José Fernandez Aguayo. *M:* Piero Piccioni. 89 (95) mins.
Lp: Cameron Mitchell, Georges Riviere, Ethel Rojo, Antonio Casas, Fernando Sancho.

One Silver Dollar (Un Dollaro Buccato). *It, Fr.* 1965.
Warner-Pathé. U.
P: Bruno Turchetto. *D:* Calvin Jackson Paget (Giorgio

Ferroni). *Sc:* George Finlay (Giorgio Stegani), Giorgio
Ferroni. *Ph:* Tony Dry (Antonio Secchi). *M:* Gianni Ferrio.
95 mins.
Lp: Montgomery Wood (Giuliano Gemma), Evelyn Stewart
(Ida Galli).

Seven Guns for the MacGregors (7 Pistole per il
MacGregor). *It, Sp.* 1965.
Columbia. A.
D: Frank Grafield (Franco Giraldi). *Sc:* Vincent Eagle
(Enzo dell' Aquila), Fernando Lion (Fernando di Leo),
David Moreno, Duccio Tessari. *Ph:* Alejandro Ulloa.
M: Ennio Morricone. *Md:* Bruno Nicolai. 90 (95) mins.
Lp: Robert Woods, Manny Zarzo (Manolo Zarzo),
Fernando Sancho.

1968
Bandidos *(alt. It. title:* Crepo Tue . . . che Vivo). *It, Sp.*
1967.
Butcher's. X.
P: Solly V. Bianco. *D:* Max Dillmann (Massimo Dallamano)
Ph: Emilio Foriscot. *M:* Egisto Macchi. 94 mins.
Lp: Enrico Maria Salerno, Terry Jenkins, Venatino Venatini.

Fort Yuma Gold (Per Pochi Dollari Ancora). *It, Fr, Sp.*
1966.
Gala. X.
P: Edmondo Amati. *D:* Calvin Jackson Paget (Giorgio
Ferroni). *Ph:* Rafael Pacheco. *M:* Ennio Morricone, Gianni
Ferrio. 100 mins.
Lp: Montgomery Wood (Giuliano Gemma), Dan Vadis,
Sophie Daumier, Angel del Pozo.

For a Dollar in the Teeth (Un Dollaro Tra i Denti).
It, USA. 1966.
Golden Era. X.
P: Carlo Infascelli. *D:* Luigi Vanzi. *Ph:* Marcello
Masciocchi. *M, Md:* Benedetto Ghiglia. 84 (96) mins.
Lp: Tony Antony, Frank Wolff, Gia Sandri.

The Good, the Bad, and the Ugly (Il Buono, Il Brutto, Il
Cattivo). *It, W. Germ, Sp.* 1966.
United Artists. X.
P: Alberto Grimaldi. *D:* Sergio Leone. *Sc:* Sergio Leone,
Luciano Vincenzoni. *Ph:* Tonino Delli Colli. *M:* Ennio
Morricone. *Md:* Bruno Nicolai. 148 (180) mins.
Lp: Clint Eastwood, Lee Van Cleef, Eli Wallach, Aldo
Giuffré, Mario Brega.

Hate for Hate (Odio per Odio). *It.* 1967.
MGM. A.
P: Italo Zingarelli. *D:* Domenico Paolella. *Sc:* Bruno
Corbucci, Fernando di Leo, Domenico Paolella. *Ph:*
Alejandro Ulloa. *M, Md:* Willy Brezza. 79 (100) mins.
Lp: Antonio Sabato, John Ireland, Fernando Sancho.

My Name is Pecos (Mio Nome é Pecos). *It.* 1966.
Golden Era. X.
P: Franco Palombi. *D:* Maurizio Lucidi. *Ph:* Franco Villa.
M: Lallo Gori. 83 mins.
Lp: Robert Woods, Lucia Modugno, Peter Carsten.

Ringo and His Golden Pistol (Johnny Oro). *It.* 1966.
MGM. U.
P: Joseph Fryd. *D:* Sergio Corbucci. *Sc:* Adriano Bolzoni,
Franco Rossetti. *Ph:* Riccardo Pallotini. *M:* Carlo Savina.
88 mins.
Lp: Mark Damon, Valeria Fabrizi, Ettore Manni.

$10,000 Dollars Blood Money (10,000 Dollari per un
Massacro). *It.* 1966.
Golden Era. X.
P: Mino Loy. *D:* Romolo Guerrieri. *Ph:* Federico Zanni.
M: Nora Orlandi. 97 mins.
Lp: Gary Hudson (Gianni Garko), Claudio Camaso,
Adriana Ambesi, Fernando Sancho.

The Tramplers (Gli Uomini del Passo Pessante). *It.* 1966.
Planet. A.
P: Joseph Levine, Alvaro Mancori. *D:* Albert Band (Alfredo
Antonini). *Sc:* Ugo Liberatore, Alfredo Antonini. *Ph:*
Alvaro Mancore. *M:* Angelo Francesco Lavagnino. 97
(105) mins.
Lp: Gordon Scott, Joseph Cotten, James Mitchum, Franco
Nero.

1969
The Big Gundown (La Resa dei Conti). *It, Sp.* 1966.
Columbia. A.
P: Alberto Grimaldi. *D:* Sergio Sollima. *Sc:* Sergio Donati,
Sergio Sollima from a story by Franco Solinas & Fernando
Moranda. *Ph:* Carlo Carlini. *M:* Ennio Morricone. *Md:*
Bruno Nicolai. 84 (105) mins.
Lp: Lee Van Cleef, Tomas Milian, Walter Barnes, Fernando
Sancho, Nieves Navarro.

A Bullet for the General (Quein Sabe?). *It.* 1966.
Warner-Pathé. X.
P: Bino Masini. *D:* Damiano Damiani. *Sc:* Salvatore Laurani.
Dialogue adapter: Franco Solinas. *Ph:* Tony Secchi. *M:* Luis
Enriquez Bacalov. *M. supervisor:* Ennio Morricone. 77 (135)
mins.
Lp: Gian-Maria Volonté, Lou Castel, Martine Beswick,
Klaus Kinsky.

Dead or Alive (Escondido). *It, USA.* 1967.
Columbia. X.
P: Albert Band (Alfredo Antonini). *D:* Franco Giraldi.
Sc: Ugo Liberatore, Luis Garfinkle, Alfredo Antonini. *Ph:*
Alace Parolini. *M:* Carlo Rustichelli. *Md:* Bruno Nicolai.
89 mins.
Lp: Alex Cord, Robert Ryan, Arthur Kennedy, Nicoletta
Machiavelli, Mario Brega.

Death Rides a Horse (Da Uomo a Uomo). *It.* 1967.
United Artists. A.
P: Alfredo Sasne, Henryk Chrosicki. *D:* Guilio Petroni.
Sc: Luciano Vincenzoni, Antonio Margharetti. *Ph:* Carlo
Carlini. *M:* Ennio Morricone. 115 mins. Cut.
Lp: Lee Van Cleef, John Phillip Law, Anthony Dawson
(Antonio Margharetti), Mario Brega.

Djurado. *It.* 1966.
Golden Era. X.
D: Gianni Narzisi. *Sc:* William Azella, Gianni Narzisi.
M: Gianni Ferrio. 78 mins.
Lp: Montgomery Clark (Dante Posani), Scilla Gabel, Luis
Induni, Margaret Lee.

Face to Face (Faccia a Faccia). *It, Sp.* 1967.
Butcher's. A.
P: Alberto Grimaldi. *D:* Sergio Sollima. *Sc:* Sergio Donati,
Sergio Sollima. *Ph:* Rafael Pacheco. *M:* Ennio Morricone.
102 (110) mins.
Lp: Gian-Maria Volonté, Tomas Milian, William Berger.

Find a Place to Die (Joe, Cercati un Posto per Morire).
It. 1968.
Miracle. X.
P: Hugo Fregonese. *D:* Anthony Ascott (Giuliano
Carmineo). *Sc:* Ralph Grave. *Ph:* Riccardo Pallottini.
M, Md: Gianni Ferrio. 90 mins. Cut.
Lp: Jeffrey Hunter, Pascale Petit, Giovanni Pallovicino,
Pierro Lulli.

Five Giants from Texas (I Cinque della Vendetta). *It, Sp.*
1966.
Golden Era. X.
P: Roberto Capitani, Aldo Ricci. *D:* Aldo Florio. *Ph:*
Victor Montreal. *M:* Franco Salina. *Md:* Luigi Zetto. 101
mins.
Lp: Guy Madison, Monica Randall, Vidal Molino.

Gringo (or) **Gunfight at Red Sands** (Duello nel Texas).
Sp, It. 1963.
British Lion. A.
D: Riccardo Blasco. *Sc:* Alfred Band (Alfredo Antonini).
Ph: Jack Dalmas (Massimo Dallamano). *M:* Dan Savio
(Ennio Morricone). *Md:* J. R. Blasco, Leo Nichols (Ennio
Morricone). 86 (95) mins.
Lp: Richard Harrison, Giacomo Rossi Stuart.

The Hellbenders (I Crudeli). *It, Sp.* 1966.
Avco Embassy. X.
P: Albert Band (Alfredo Antonini). *D:* Sergio Corbucci.
Sc: Albert Band, Ugo Liberatore from a story by Ugo
Liberatore and José G. Naesso. *Ph:* Enzo Barboni. *M:* Leo
Nichols (Ennio Morricone). 92 (95) mins.
Lp: Joseph Cotten, Norma Bengell, Julian Mateos, Gino
Pernice, Angel Aranda, Al Mulock, Aldo Sambrell, Enzo
Girolami.

Kill Them All and Come Back Alone (Ammazzali Tutti e
Torno Solo). *It, Sp.* 1968.
P: Edmondo Amati. *D:* Enzo G. Castellari (Enzo Girolami).
Sc: Tito Carpi, Enzo Girolami. *Ph:* Alejandro Ulloa.
M: Francesco de Masi. 98 (100) mins.
Lp: Chuck Connors, Frank Wolff, Franco Citti.

Once Upon a Time in the West (C'era una Volta il West).
It. 1968.
Paramount. A.
P: Bino Cicogna. *D:* Sergio Leone. *Sc:* Sergio Leone,
Sergio Donati, Bernardo Bertolucci. *M:* Ennio Morricone.
144 (165) mins.
Lp: Claudia Cardinale, Henry Fonda, Jason Robards,
Frank Wolff, Gabrielle Ferzetti.

A Professional Gun (Il Mercanario). *It, Sp.* 1968.
United Artists. A.
P: Alberto Grimaldi. *D:* Sergio Corbucci. *Sc:* Luciano
Vincenzoni, Sergio Corbucci from a story by Franco Solinas
and Giorgio Alorio. *Ph:* Alejandro Ulloa. *M:* Ennio

Morricone and Bruno Nicolai. *Md:* Bruno Nicolai.
105 mins. Cut.
Lp: Franco Nero, Tony Musante, Jack Palance.

Revenge at El Paso (Il Quattro dell' Ave Maria). *It.* 1968.
P: Bino Cicogno. *D:* Giuseppe Colizzi. *Sc:* Giuseppe
Colizzi. *Ph:* Marcello Masciocchi. *M:* Carlo Rustichelli.
102 (137) mins.
Lp: Terence Hill (Mario Girotti), Bud Spencer (Carlo
Pedersoli), Eli Wallach, Brock Peters, Kevin McCarthy.

Seven from Texas (Camino del Sur). *Sp, It.* 1964.
Cinecenta. U.
D: J. L. Romero Marchent. *Ph:* Rafael Pacheco. *M:* Riz
Ortolani. 91 (94) mins.
Lp: Robert Hundar (Claudio Undari), Gloria Milland.

Today It's Me . . . Tomorrow You! (Oggi a Me . . . Domani
a Te!). *It.* 1968.
Miracle. X.
D: Tonino Cervi. *Sc:* Dario Argento, Tonino Cervi. *Ph:*
Sergio d' Offizi. *M:* Angelo Francesco Lavagnino. 95 mins.
Lp: Montgomery Ford (Brett Halsey), Bud Spencer (Carlo
Pedersoli), William Berger, Wayde Preston, Tatsuya Nakadai.

Two Gunmen (Los Rurales de Texas). *Sp, It.* 1964.
Compton. U.
D: Anthony Greepy (Primo Zeglio). *Sc:* Jesus Navarro,
Primo Zeglio. *Ph:* Alfredo Fraile. *M:* Francesco de Masi.
95 mins.
Lp: Alan Scott, Suzy Anderson, George Martin (Jorge Martin).

1970
Arizona Colt. *It, Sp, Fr.* 1965.
Golden Era. X.
P: Elio Scardamaglia. *D:* Michele Lupo. *Ph:* Gugliemo
Mancori. *M:* Francesco de Masi. 104 mins.
Lp: Giuliano Gemma, Corinne Marchand, Fernando
Sancho, Nello Pazzafini, Roberto Camardiel.

The Avenger (Texas Addio). *It, Sp.* 1966.
Westland. AA.
P: Manolo Bolognini. *D:* Ferdinando Baldi. *Sc:* Franco
Rossetti, Ferdinando Baldi. *Ph:* Enzo Barboni. *M:* Anton
Abril. 92 mins.
Lp: Franco Nero, Cole Kitosh, José Suarez, Elisa Montes.

Day of Anger (I Giorni dell'Ira). *It, W. Germ.* 1967.
Warner-Pathé. X.
P: Alfonso Sansone, Enrico Chrosicki. *D:* Tonino Valerii.
Sc: Ernesto Gestaldi, Renso Genta, Tonino Valerii from the
novel *Der Tod ritt Dienstags* by Ron Barker. *Ph:* Enzo Serafini.
M: Riz Ortolani. 78 (109) mins.
Lp: Lee Van Cleef, Giuliano Gemma, Walter Rilla, Yvonne
Sanson, Al Mulock.

Django Kill! (Sei sei Vivo, Spara!). *It, Sp.* 1969.
Golden Era. X.
D: Giulio Questi. *Sc:* Giulio Questi, Franco Arcalli. *Ph:*
Franco Delli Colli. *M:* Ivan Vandor. 101 (120) mins.
Lp: Tomas Milian, Pierro Lulli, Milo Quesada, Roberto
Camardiel, Marilú Tolu, Raymond Lovelock.

The Five Man Army (Un Esercito di 5 Uomini). *It.* 1969.
MGM. A.
D: Don Taylor. *Sc:* Dario Argento, Marc Richards. *Ph:* Enzo
Barboni. *M:* Ennio Morricone. *Md:* Bruno Nicolai. 105 mins
Lp: Peter Graves, Bud Spencer, Nino Castelnuovo, James
Daly, Tetsuro Tamba.

Navajo Joe (Un Dollaro a Testa). *It, Sp.* 1966.
United Artists. X.
D: Sergio Corbucci. *Sc:* Dean Craig (Mario Pierotti),
Fernando di Leo from a story by Ugo Pirro. *Ph:* Silvano
Ippolito. *M:* Leo Nichols (Ennio Morricone). 90 mins. Cut.
Lp: Burt Reynolds, Aldo Sambrell, Nicoletta Machiavelli,
Fernando Rey.

No Room to Die (Una Lunga Fila di Croci). *It.* 1969.
Miracle. A.
P: Gabriele Crisanti. *D:* Sergio Garrone. *Sc:* Sergio Garrone
Ph: Franco Villa. *M:* Vasco and Mancuso. 88 (93) mins.
Lp: Anthony Steffen (Antonio de Teffé), William Berger,
Nicoletta Machiavelli, Mario Brega.

Poker with Pistols (Un Poker di Pistole). *It.* 1967.
Golden Era. A.
D: Joseph Warren (Giuseppe Vari). *Sc:* Augusto Caminoto,
Fernando di Leo. *Ph:* Angelo Lotti. *M:* Lallo Gori. 86 mins.
Lp: George Eastman (Luigi Montefiore), Annabella
Incontrera, George Hilton.

The Return of Ringo (Il Ritorno di Ringo). *It, Sp.* 1965.
Golden Era. A.

D : Duccio Tessari. Sc : Duccio Tessari, Fernando di Leo.
Ph : Francisco Marin. M : Ennio Morricone. 96 mins.
Lp : Giuliano Gemma, Fernando Sancho, Hally Hammond
(Lorella de Luca), Niêves Navarro, Antonio Casas,
George Martin.

Wanted. It. 1968.
Golden Era. X.
D : Calvin Jackson Padget (Giorgio Ferroni). Sc : Fernando
di Leo, Augosto Finocchi. Ph : Tony Secchi. M : Gianni
Ferrio. 104 mins.
Lp : Giuliano Gemma, Teresa Gimpera, Serge Marquand.

1971
Beyond the Law (Al di lá della Legge). It. W. Germ. 1967.
Rank. U.
P : Alfonso Sansone, Enrico Chroscicki. D : Giorgio Stegani.
Sc : Warren Kiefer, Fernando di Leo, Mino Roli, Giorgio
Stegani from a story by Warren Kiefer. Ph : Enzo Serafin.
M : Riz Ortolani. 85 (110) mins.
Lp : Lee Van Cleef, Antonio Sabato, Gordon Mitchell,
Lionel Stander.

Bury Them Deep (All' Ultimo Sangue). It. 1968.
E. J. Fancey. AA.
D : John Byrd (Paolo Moffa). Ph : Franco Villa. M : Nico
Fidenco. Md : Willy Brezza. 91 (100) mins.
Lp : Craig Hill, Ettore Manni, Kenn Wood.

Death Sentence (Sentenza di Morte). It. 1967.
Miracle. X.
D : Mario Lanfranchi. Sc : Mario Lanfranchi. Ph : Tony
Secchi. M : Gianni Ferrio. 82 (90) mins.
Lp : Robin Clarke, Richard Conte, Enrico Maria Salerno,
Adolfo Celi, Tomas Milian.

For a Few Bullets More (Vado . . . l'Ammazo e Torno).
It. 1967.
Gala. A.
D : Enzo G. Gastellari (Enzo Girolami). Sc : Giovanni
Simmonelli, Enzo G. Castellari. Ph : Giovanni Bergamini.
M :.Francesco De Masi. 100 mins.
Lp : George Hilton, Edd Byrnes, Gilbert Roland.

The Price of Power (Il Prezzo del Potere). It, Sp. 1969.
Golden Era. X.
D : Tonino Valerii. Sc : Massimo Patrizi. Ph : Stelvio Massi.
M : Luis Enriquez Bacalov. 96 (122) mins.

Lp : Giuliano Gemma, Van Johnson, Warren Vanders,
Fernando Rey.

Sabata (Ehi, Amico . . . c'e Sabata, hai chiuso!). It. 1969.
United Artists. AA.
P : Alberto Grimaldi. D : Frank Kramer (Gianfranco Parolini).
Sc : Gianfranco Parolini, Renato Izzo. Ph : Sandro Mancori.
M : Marcello Giombini. 106 mins.
Lp : Lee Van Cleef, William Berger, Pedro Sanchez, Franco
Ressel, Linda Veras, Gianni Rizzo.

The Unholy Four (Ciak Mull, l'Uomo della Vendetta).
It. 1969.
Eagle. A.
P : Manolo Bolognini. D : E. B. Clucher (Enzo Barboni).
Sc : Franco Rossetti, Mario di Nardo from a story by
Franco Rossetti. Ph : Mario Mantuori. M : Riz Ortolani.
96 mins.
Lp : Leonard Mann, Woody Strode, Helmut Schneider,
Evelyn Stewart, Luca Montefiore.

Vengeance is Mine (Quei Disperati che Puzzano di Sudore
et di Morte). It. Sp. 1969.
Golden Era. X.
P : Elio Scardamaglia, Ugo Guerra. D : Julio Buchs. Sc :
José Luis Martinez Mollo, Frederico de Urnutia, Ugo
Guerra, Julio Buchs. Ph : Francisco Sempere. M, Md : Gianni
Ferrio. 100 mins. Cut.
Lp : George Hilton, Ernest Borgnine, Alberto de Mendoza.

1972
Blood River (Dio Perdona . . . Io No!). It, Sp. 1967.
Border. X.
P : Enzo D' Ambrosio. D : Giuseppe Colizzi. Sc : Giuseppe
Colizzi. Ph : Alfo Contini. M : Angel Oliver Pino (Carlo
Rustichelli). 97 (115) mins.
Lp : Terence Hill (Mario Girotti), Bud Spencer (Carlo
Pedersoli), Frank Wolff.

The Boldest Job in the West (or) **Nevada** (El Mas
Fabulosi Golpe del Far West). Sp, It, Fr. 1971.
Gala. A.
D : José Antonio de la Loma. Ph : Hans Burmann, Antonio
Millan. M : Gianni Marchetti. Md : Stelvio Cipriani. 101 mins.
Lp : Mark Edwards, Carmen Sevilla, Fernando Sancho.

Compañeros (Vamos a Matar, Compañeros!). It, Sp, W.
Germ. 1970.

Twentieth Century Fox. X.
P: Alberto Grimaldi. *D*: Sergio Corbucci. *Sc*: Dino Maiuri, Massimo de Rita, Fritz Ebert, Sergio Corbucci from an idea by Sergio Corbucci. *Ph*: Alejandro Ulloa. *M*: Ennio Morricone. *Md*: Bruno Nicolai. 118 mins.
Lp: Franco Nero, Tomas Milian, Jack Palance, Fernando Rey.

Dead Men Ride (Il Sole Sotta Terra). *It*, *Sp*. 1971.
British Lion. X.
D: Aldo Florio. *Sc*: Aldo Florio, Bruno di Geronimo, E. M. Brochero. *Ph*: Emilio Foriscot. *M*: Bruno Nicolai. 94 (101) mins.
Lp: Fabio Testi, Charo Lopez, Ben Carro.

A Fistful of Dynamite (Giú La Testa). *It*. 1971.
United Artists. AA.
P: Fulvio Morsella. *D*: Sergio Leone. *Sc*: Luciano Vincenzoni, Sergio Leone from a story by Sergio Leone. *Ph*: Giuseppe Ruzzolini. *Second Unit Ph*: Franco Delli Colli. *M*: Ennio Morricone. 138 (150) mins.
Lp: Rod Steiger, James Coburn, Romolo Valli.

The Longest Hunt (Spara Gringo Spara). *It*. 1968.
Tigon. A.
P: William Sachs. *D*: Frank B. Corlish (Bruno Corbucci). *Sc*: Dean Whitcomb (Bruno Corbucci), Mario Amendolo. *Ph*: Fausto Zuccoli. *M*, *Md*: Richard Ira Silver (Sante M. Romitelli). 89 (100) mins.
Lp: Brian Kelly, Frank Munroe (Fabrizio Moroni), Keenan Wynn, Folco Lulli, Erica Blanc.

The Magnificent Bandits (O Cangaceiro). *It*, *Sp*. 1969.
Golden Era. AA.
D: Giovanni Fago. *Sc*: Giovanni Fago. *Ph*: Alejandro Ulloa. *M*: Riz Ortolani and Brasilian folk songs. 90 (102) mins.
Lp: Tomas Milian, Ugo Pagliani, Eduardo Fajuardo.

The Return of Sabata (E' Tornato Sabata . . . Hai Chiuso un' Altro Volto). *It*, *Fr*, *W. Germ*. 1971.
United Artists. X.
P: Alberto Grimaldi. *D*: Frank Kramer (Gianfranco Parolini). *Sc*: Renato Izzo, Gianfranco Parolini. *Ph*: Sandro Mancori. *M*: Marcello Giombini. 88 (107) mins.
Lp: Lee Van Cleef, Reiner Schöne, Annabella Incontrera, Gianni Rizzo, Pedro Sanchez (Ignazio Spalla).

Vengeance (Joko, Invoco Dio . . . e Muori). *It*, *W. Germ*. 1968.
MGM-EMI. X.
D: Anthony Dawson (Antonio Margheretti). *Sc*: Antonio Margheretti, Renato Savino. *Ph*: Riccardo Pallotini. *M*: Carlo Savina. 81 (100) mins.
Lp: Richard Harrison, Claudio Camaso.

1973
The Big and the Bad (Si Puo Fare . . . Amigo).
It, *Fr*, *Sp*. 1971.
MGM-EMI. U.
P: Alfonso Sasone. *D*: Maurizio Lucidi. *Sc*: Rafael Azcona. *Ph*: Aldo Tonti. *M*, *Md*: Luis Enriquez Bacalov. 84 mins.
Lp: Bud Spencer, Jack Palance, Francisco Rabal.

The Bounty Hunters (Indio Black, Sai Che Ti Dico: Sei un Gran Figlio di . . .). *It*. 1970.
United Artists. A.
P: Albert Grimaldi. *D*: Frank Kramer (Gianfranco Parolini). *Sc*: Renato Izzo, Gianfranco Parolini. *Ph*: Sandro Mancori. *M*: Bruno Nicolai. 106 mins.
Lp: Yul Brynner, Dean Reed, Pedro Sanchez (Ignazio Spallo), Gerard Herter.

Deaf Smith and Johnny Ears (Los Amigos). *It*. 1972.
MGM-EMI. AA.
P: Joseph Janni, Luciano Perugo. *D*: Paolo Cavara. *Sc*: Harry Essex, Oscar Saul, Paolo Cavara, Lucia Drudi, Augusto Finocchi from a story by Oscar Saul and Harry Essex. *Ph*: Tonino Delli Colli. *M*, *Md*: Daniele Patucchi. 92 mins.
Lp: Anthony Quinn, Franco Nero, Pamela Tiffin.

Drop Them or I'll Shoot (Le Spécialiste). *Fr*, *W. Germ*, *It*. 1969.
Golden Era. X.
P, *D*: Sergio Corbucci. *Sc*: Sergio Corbucci, Sabatine Griffi. *Ph*: Dario di Palma. *M*: Francesco Lavagnino. 90 (98) mins.
Lp: Johnny Hallyday, Sylvie Fennec, Françoise Fabian, Serge Marquand, Mario Adorf.

He Who Shoots First (Django Spara per Primo) *It*. 1966.
Gala. AA.
P: Edmondo Amati. *D*: Alberto de Martino. *Ph*: Riccardo Pallotini. *M*: Bruno Nicolai. 95 mins.

: Glenn Saxon, Fernando Sancho, Evelyn Stewart.

an of the East (. . . e pri lo chiamavono Il Magnifico)
Fr. 1972.
nited Artists. A.
Albert Grimaldi. D : E. B. Clucher (Enzo Barboni).
: Enzo Barboni Ph : Aldo Giordini. M : Guido & Maurizio
Angelis. 125 mins.
: Terence Hill, Gregory Walcott, Harry Carey.

e Man Who Killed Billy the Kid (El Hombre que
tao Billy el Niño). Sp, It. 1967.
hard Schulman Entertainments. A.
Silvo Battistini. D : Julio Buchs. Sc : Julio Buchs, Federico
Urrutia, Carlo Vero from a story by Julio Buchs, José
lorqui, Federico de Urrutia. Ph : Miguel Milo.
Md : Gianni Ferrio. 86 mins.
Peter Lee Lawrence (Karl Hirenbach), Fausto Tozzi.

4
dman. USA, It. 1971.
-Rank. X.
ony Antony, Saul Swimmer. D : Ferdinando Baldi. Sc :
y Antony, Piero Anchisi, Vincenzo Cerami from a story
ony Antony. Ph : Riccardo Pallotini. M, Md : Stelvio
iani. 96 (105) mins.
Tony Antony, Ringo Starr, Agneta Eckemyr, Lloyd
sta, Magda Kanopka.

Con Men (Te Deum). It. Sp. 1973.
Rank. A.
nzo G. Castellari. Sc : Enzo G. Castellari, Gianni
nelli, Tito Carpi. Ph : Manolo Rojas. M : Guido &
rizio De Angelis. 91 (99) mins.
ack Palance, Timothy Brent, Lionel Stander.

and Lester, Two Brothers in a Place called Trinity
Fratelli in un posto chiamato Trinità). It. 1972.
ay. X.
chard Harrison, Fernando Piazza. D : James London.
enzo Senti from a story by Richard Harrison. M :
Savina. 97 mins.
ichard Harrison, Donald O'Brien, Anne Zinneman.

ason to Live, a Reason to Die (Una Ragione per
e una per Morire). It, Fr, Sp, W. Germ. 1972.
. AA.
chael Billingsley. D : Tonino Valerii. Sc : Tonino

Valerii, Ernesto Gastaldi. Ph : Alejandro Ulloa. M : Riz
Ortolani. 91 (96) mins.
Lp : James Coburn, Telly Savalas, Bud Spencer.

Trinity is Still My Name (Continuavamo a Chiamarlo
Trinity). It. 1971.
Avco Embassy. U.
P : Italo Zingarelli. D : E. B. Clucher. Sc : E. B. Clucher.
Ph : Aldo Giordani. M : G & M De Angelis. 90 (121) mins.
Lp : Terence Hill, Bud Spencer, Harry Carey.

1975
Blood Money. Hong Kong, It, Sp, USA. 1974.
Columbia-Warner. X.
D : Anthony M. Dawson (Antonio Margheriti). Sc : Barth

Jules Sussman. Ph : Alejandro Ulloa. M : Carlo Savina.
100 mins.
Lp : Lee Van Cleef, Lo Lieh, Karen Yeh.

To Kill or to Die (Il Mio Nome é Shanghai Joe). It. 1973.
Miracle. X.
D : Mario Caiano. Sc : Mario Caiano, Fabrizio Trifone Trecca.
Ph : Guglielmo Mancori. M : Bruno Nicolai. 98 mins.
Lp : Chen Lee, Carla Romanelli, Klaus Kinsky.

Information on accessibility and supply of soundtracks
mentioned in this book may be obtained from
Michael Jones
406 Brockley Road
London SE4